F

THESE OLD STONE WALLS

By PHILLIPS RUSSELL

The Chapel Hill Historical Society

Copyright © 1972 by
The Chapel Hill Historical Society
Second Printing 1973

Third Printing 1983
Manufactured in The United States of America
Printed by the Greensboro Printing Company
Greensboro, North Carolina
Library of Congress Catalog Card No. 73-151830

A publication of

*To make available to present and future genera-
tions those works that will enrich the perception of
Chapel Hill and its environs, preserve those aspects
of its heritage that can be compressed between covers,
and sustain the traditions for which the village and
its people have so long been known.*

Order from
The Chapel Hill Historical Society
Post Office Box 503
Chapel Hill, North Carolina 27514

These Old Stone Walls

By Phillips Russell

Who could tell you better than Phillips Russell what has happened through the years in Chapel Hill behind "these old stone walls?"

Born in Rockingham, N. C., in 1884 and educated at the University of North Carolina in Chapel Hill, where he taught creative writing for 25 years, Phillips Russell was familiar with both the historical facts and the romantic legends of Chapel Hill.

In this book he tells about the first chapel for which "Chapel Hill" was named; about the Revolutionary War General William R. Davie, who may or may not have hitched his horse to the Davie Poplar; about Dr. Elisha Mitchell, who brought the idea of stone walls down from New England and gave his name to our Mount Mitchell; about whether Senator Thomas Hart Benton was really expelled from the University of North Carolina for stealing from his classmates; about the first President, Joseph Caldwell, who used to chase students across the campus if he caught them in mischief; about black November Caldwell, coachman to the President, and the black poet, George M. Horton, who wrote love verses for the students to send their sweethearts.

He tells about the "po' boy painter" who walked to Chapel Hill from Burke County, about the hexagon-shaped house designed by "the only professor ever fired from the faculty because of his opinions," about the alleged duel fought at the site of Gimghoul Castle, and about the portraits of Martha and Varina Mason and why they hang in a University hall.

Phillips Russell not only tells you what you always wanted

to know about Chapel Hill — but even answers questions you did not know how to ask.

Recipient of the North Carolina Award for literature in 1968, Professor Russell was the author of numerous books, including *The Woman Who Rang the Bell, Red Tiger, The Glittering Century, Emerson, The Wisest American, John Paul Jones, Man of Action* and *North Carolina in the Revolutionary War.*

Photo by Sam Hood

Books by Phillips Russell

Benjamin Franklin, the First Civilized American

John Paul Jones, Man of Action

Emerson, the Wisest American

Harvesters

William the Conqueror

Red Tiger

Fumbler

The Glittering Century

The Woman Who Rang the Bell

North Carolina in the Revolutionary War

Illustrations

Contents

Most of the portraits contained in this volume were supplied by the Carolina Collection of the University of North Carolina Library.

The picture of the old stone walls near the President's House was taken especially for the outside cover by Rich Beckman, photojournalism lecturer in the School of Journalism at the University of North Carolina.

A Hill and a Chapel

On the crest of the eminence now occupied by the Carolina Inn, which is owned and operated by the University of North Carolina through the gift of the late John Sprunt Hill and his family, there once stood in pre-Revolutionary War times a chapel of the Church of England. The community as a whole then seems to have been known by the name of New Hope, which name still clings to the Presbyterian Church about eight miles north of the village, and to the creek crossing the road between Chapel Hill and Durham. Tradition says the locality was known as the Hill of New Hope Chapel, or simply as New Hope Chapel Hill. In the course of time the first two words became confined to the rural community mentioned, so that the village itself gradually acquired the last two words, hence finally becoming known simply as Chapel Hill.

The chapel on the hill, whose minister was "Parson" George Micklejohn, was established at the point where two great roads crossed. North and south ran the road over which hogsheads of tobacco and droves of pigs were forwarded between Pittsboro, N. C., and Petersburg, Virginia. East and west ran the road connecting the eastern market towns of New Bern and Fayetteville (which sold salt and bought deerskins) with the more western centers at Salisbury and Wachovia.

In 1789 North Carolina, which had been one of George III's thirteen American colonies, ratified the Union of States. On December 18, 1776, it had adopted a State constitution bearing these words: "All useful learning shall be duly encouraged and promoted in one or more universities." A month after the State had adopted the Constitution it chartered the University of North Carolina on December 11, 1789. This was largely at the instance of General William R. Davie, cavalry leader and supply officer to General Nathanael Greene in the Revolutionary War, and later envoy to France, who is thus described: "A tall, elegant man in his person, graceful and commanding in his manners . . . his voice was mellow . . . his mind comprehensive."

On October 12, 1793, the cornerstone of the first building, "Old East," was laid. Sixteen months later, February 12, 1795, the first student, Hinton James of Wilmington, walked into the one-building university and registered.

Thus the University of North Carolina began its long career as an institution to encourage and promote "all useful learning." Around it and the village which developed with it have grown up countless tales. This book recounts a few of them.

A Tree and a Soldier

In the upper part of the northern quadrangle of the campus stands Chapel Hill's venerated tree, the Davie poplar. Not actually a poplar but a tulip tree, it was named for "the Father of the University," Brig. Gen. William Richardson Davie, partisan horseman in the Revolutionary War, governor, lawyer, legislator and diplomat.

How did his name become attached to a tree? Around that question are gathered many legends. The most picturesque is that General Davie, member of a committee in search of a site for the University, stopped his horse for a drink from a spring in the woods not far from New Hope Chapel and before remounting stuck his switch in the ground. And from this switch sprang the Davie Poplar. That is the story most treasured by University students. But history is silent on the subject. The General himself never left a recorded word about it, and Battle, Mrs. Spencer, Henderson and Connor, the leading campus historians, merely hint that Davie and his party stopped at the spot for rest and refreshment and impressed by the beauty and health of the surroundings, declared the University should be established here.

The General himself took no credit for founding of the University. The gist of the bill leading to its birth he attributed to the Rev. Dr. Samuel Eusebius McCorkle, its shaping to Judge Spruce Macay, and its introduction to William Sharpe, a trustee for 18 years. Sharpe on Nov. 8, 1784, introduced in the House of Commons a bill to establish "a University in this State to be distinguished by the title of the President and Trustees of the North Carolina University."

All of these men were from Rowan County, whose county seat, Salisbury, produced many State leaders. Dr. McCorkle was an active Presbyterian divine. Judge Macay was the teacher of Andrew Jackson and of Davie himself, and Sharpe was a surveyor and lawyer who had been a member of the Continental Congress 1779-81. No action was taken on his bill, due in Davie's words to "multiplicity of claims and an empty till."

That the Father of the University could have a light touch in his letters is indicated by a note he wrote to Judge Macay on Sept. 3, 1793, saying: "As one who once sat at the feet of Gamaliel in the intermissions between tours in the field, I write to press for your attendance at Chapel Hill in Orange on Oct. 10 (actually the 12th) laying of a corner stone, great doings of the Masonic brethren, with your correspondent wielding a silver trowel and setting a stone in mortar."

Following Sharpe's ignored bill, Davie himself had introduced at a meeting of the Legislature in Fayetteville in 1789 a bill with a Jeffersonian touch saying: "Whereas in all well regulated Governments, it is the indispensable duty of every Legislature to consult the Happiness of a rising generation and endeavor to fit them for an honourable discharge of the social duties of life, by paying the strictest attention to their education. . ."[1] This was the second attempt to establish a University through legislative channels. It is significant that Davie's list of suggested trustees began

[1] Robinson, *William R. Davie.*

with Gov. Samuel Johnston and Justice James Iredell, who both had Federalist views in opposition to Thomas Jefferson's democratic doctrines.

At this time Davie was in the House of Commons as member for the town of Halifax. On Nov. 6, 1789, he wrote Iredell: "We have gone on smoothly as yet . . . The University bill will certainly pass . . . The Anti's attempted to put Spencer upon us, but the business was better managed. The calculations were greatly in favor of the Constitution."[2] The reference here is to the battle over the ratification of the United States Constitution, North Carolina having held out against it. It passed. Spencer was Judge Samuel Spencer of Anson County, Superior Court judge and University trustee. The General was here again betraying his strong Federalist bias in favor of a centralized government by a land-owning class. He himself owned at one time as many as 116 slaves.

A year later Davie wrote Governor Alexander Martin: "You will, I am certain, give the University every assistance in your power as a man who knows the importance of education in a country just forming its manners and its Government."[3] In this passage the General gives a hint of his realization that he and his fellow Federalists were facing a rough and untutored mass of fellow citizens belonging to a pioneer stock which eventually put Thomas Jefferson in power. In his more uneasy moments Davie called them "Jacobins" or worse, and thought they would ruin the republic.

In 1791 Davie led a drive in the Legislature that got the embryo University a loan of £1500, but only after strong

[2] *Idem.*
[3] *Idem.*

opposition from legislators who feared the Federalist leaders intended to create at Chapel Hill a political center.

Davie himself was born into a property-owning family which, though not rich, owned enough land to give it considerable standing. He was the son of English nonconformist parents, Archibald Davie and his wife, Mary Richardson, on whose tomb is engraved the Davie arms. She wrote in her Bible that the child named William Richardson Davie was born June 22, 1756, in the village of Egremont, County Cumberland, England. Mary's brother, William Richardson, had gone to America several years before. After preparing himself in Virginia for the Presbyterian ministry, he had received a call from the Waxhaws below Charlotte, N. C., and taken the church in St. Mark's Parish, Craven County, South Carolina. The Scottish, Irish, and German settlers there had found the land good and become prosperous. The Rev. William Richardson, on attaining some prosperity himself, invited young Davie's parents to join him, and thither they sailed and took up land in 1766.

Young Davie received some schooling at Charlotte and in 1774 attended the College of New Jersey, which later became Princeton University. He was reading law under Judge Spruce Macay at Salisbury when in 1777 the war for independence gripped him and he joined a force of mounted volunteers commanded by Gen. Allen Jones of Northampton County, whose daughter he later married.

In 1779 Davie was commissioned a lieutenant of horse and saw strenuous activity throughout the Revolution. He was in his hottest battle under Gen. Benjamin Lincoln at Stono where he was wounded in the thigh and fell from his horse. He was rescued by an unknown private. During a long convalescence Davie resumed his study of law and was licensed in November, 1779. But the next year he was back in the war as head of his own troop, which did major service in scouting and guerrilla activity, particularly at Charlotte when Cornwallis invaded North Carolina. In fact, he was very much on a par with the more famous partisan leaders, Marion, Sumter, and Pickens.

When General Greene came south his army suffered from lack of supplies and he prevailed on Davie to become commissary general. In this thankless office Davie labored for the rest of the war, and became not only Greene's reliable supply officer but his confidant. After the war Davie asked Greene for a certificate of service. This never came.

In April, 1782, Davie wed Sarah, 19 years old, the daughter of Brig. Gen. Allen Jones of Halifax, N. C. At the war's end he started building his home, "Loretta," in Halifax and took possession in 1785. The year before he had been elected to the House of Commons.

It was as a member of the legislature that Davie began to urge the rise and financing of the University, which managed to open its doors to students in 1795. In that year he wrote to Treasurer John Haywood a bit of philosophy which arose in consequence of a death in Haywood's family.

"My dear sir: I regret exceedingly the various causes which procured your absence from the board. However, as the Arabs say, 'God would have it so,' and men must submit. Under misfortunes like yours there is no comfort, because nothing can be substituted; the only resource for the human mind in such cases is in a kind of philosophic fortitude, the certain result of time, reason and reflection."[4]

For 18 years from this time the General was the University's guide and counsellor. Its first honorary degree of Doctor of Laws was given to him. Strange to say, he opposed the teaching of dramatics there, but favored dancing.

In 1798 he was appointed a brigadier general, later a major general, in the United States Army. In the same year he was elected Governor of North Carolina. He resigned that office to join a commission of three appointed by President John Adams to go to France and end a quarrel with Napoleon's government. On his return to Halifax he found the political atmosphere so much changed that he resolved to move to South Carolina. He met defeat in a campaign for Congress and this finally disillusioned him with North Carolina voters. But even on his retirement to South Carolina he kept up a lively interest in Chapel Hill, where in fact he had bought lots. His was undoubtedly the chief influence that brought Joseph Caldwell, a Princeton graduate, there as the University's first President.

Davie never recovered his spirits after the defeat and disappearance of the Federalist Party dating from 1800, and was convinced that under Jefferson and his successors the country was going to the dogs. For some months he suffered from rheumatism and a liver disorder. On Nov. 5, 1820, he died at his estate, "Tivoli," and was buried in the Old Waxhaw Presbyterian churchyard. His estate included 116 slaves, estimated to be worth $32,000.

In 1827 Judge Archibald D. Murphey wrote that the General was "a tall, elegant man in his person, graceful

[4] Robinson, *Idem.*

and commanding in his manners." The same authority said that on the occasion in 1791 when the General asked £5,000 of the General Assembly for the embryo University: "I have the most vivid recollection of the greatness of his manner and the powers of his eloquence."

Gen. Davie was typical of the colonial proprietors and land owners who furnished the American leaders and spokesmen of the Revolutionary War, which was in part a rebellion against the trade strangulation of the British government under George III. But he was superior to most of them. Without Davie's organizing and sustained work as North Carolina's commissary general, General Greene's campaign in the two Carolinas might have had a far different ending. But General Davie, able as he was, had his limitations. He had no sympathy with the delegated forms of democratic government which the nascent nation was developing and which gave power to a pioneer class of farmers and hunters. These men did not belong to the 18th century English gentry. But from their muscle and energy rose the American republic, crude, undisciplined, and powerful.

These Old Stone Walls

Characteristic of Chapel Hill are the low stone walls that run about the campus and town. The newer ones are mortared, but the older walls, weathered to a brownish grey, consist simply of field stones piled one upon the other in New England style.

These walls are indeed of New England descent. They were built largely under the eye of Dr. Elisha Mitchell, who after being graduated from Yale, came down in 1818 from his native Connecticut to make his home in Chapel Hill as a professor in the University. His chair was first that of mathematics, later of chemistry, geology and mineralogy. Dr. Mitchell was one of the first of the long line of versatile and distinguished professors who have invested Chapel Hill with a creative and zestful spirit. Nothing organic or inorganic was alien to him. He was a preacher and farmer, village commissioner and magistrate. Meantime he was teaching in three different fields, carrying on various scientific researches, and acting as the college bursar.

He was born at Washington, Conn., August 17, 1793, son of a farmer who believed in Congregational Calvinism. Young Mitchell went to Yale College at the age of 16 and studied science under Dr. Ben Silliman. To avoid frightening the orthodox, science was then disguised as Natural Philosophy. At Chapel Hill, with the same motivation, science was called Mental and Moral Philosophy. After graduation Mitchell taught in a school for girls at New London, where he found his wife. Later he was a tutor at Yale and a theological student at Andover, where he was licensed to preach. While still a student he became a friend of George E. Badger, later United States Senator and Secretary of the Navy, also a friend of Denison Olmsted, who later became his host at Chapel Hill.

The rumpled country that lies around Chapel Hill is cut by streams and ridges which Dr. Mitchell took over for scientific purposes by walking over it and exploring it yard by yard for specimens. He knew where outcropped the blue and stratified stone found in abundance near the village; where the yellow jasmine first blooms in spring; and just how many species of oaks are found within two miles of the campus.

He loved to take his students on long tramps, and could enjoy the jokes and puns of such a student wit as Zeb. B. Vance, afterwards war Governor of the State and then United States Senator. On coming to the site of Barbee's Mill one day, the student Vance asked, "Doctor, you reckon this old mill is worth a dam?" The doctor's reply is not given.

Dr. Mitchell went on walking and exploring and enjoying life to the last day of his life. Mt. Mitchell, the highest peak east of the Mississippi, is his monument, for it was there he lost his life by a fall in the course of an exploring journey one day in 1857. The Elisha Mitchell Scientific Society of the University still carries on the traditions of accurate study of nature established by him.

Dr. Mitchell's house stood where Swain Hall was later built, near the west gate of the campus, within a stone's throw of the Carolina Inn. Four of his grandchildren, who failed to survive infancy were buried, in accord with the custom of the day, at the rear of his home; and there that little graveyard stood for years, unprotected, behind Swain Hall. In its center was a little marble shaft, each face bearing the name of a child. This little graveyard was eventually run over and crushed by delivery trucks.

Dr. Mitchell's wife was Miss Maria North, daughter of a New London, Connecticut, physician. They were married at Lyme, Connecticut, in 1819. Mrs. Mitchell has left some interesting notes regarding the bridal journey south and her subsequent life in Chapel Hill.

They came down by boat to Elizabethtown, N. J., then to Trenton and Philadelphia by stage, thence by boat down the Delaware to New Castle, thence by stage to Frenchtown, down the Chesapeake to Baltimore and Norfolk, thence by stage to the Dismal Swamp where a canal boat carried them 22 miles to a point where they took a one-horse gig to a tavern, whence they reached Elizabeth City by stage. Albemarle Sound they crossed in an open rowboat. Then by way of Williamston, Tarboro, and Raleigh they reached Chapel Hill where they obtained board and lodging at the home of Professor Denison Olmsted,* who later joined the faculty at Yale. They paid him $288 a year for their "board, lodging and washing."

"Immediately after leaving Raleigh," Mrs. Mitchell wrote home, "we plunged into the woods, leaving all civilization behind us. We went through woods and more woods, taking all day for the trip, 29 miles." They arrived at Chapel Hill on December 29 when a light snow lay on the ground. Waiting students fired a volley into the air as a sign of welcome. (Students of the period went armed or kept firearms in their rooms.)

There were other signs of primitive conditions. Mrs.

---

* This house was called the Widow Puckett House and then the James Phillips House. In modern times it was occupied by Chancellor R. B. House, who, by vote of the Board of Trustees, continued in it when he became Chancellor Emeritus.

Mitchell had to send back home for thread, needles and cambric, but after settling down she found she liked Chapel Hill "far better than anticipated."

Dr. Mitchell also enjoyed the life on the young University campus, writing home: "The prosperity of the University is dearer to me than any earthly thing besides my wife and children." But his post as Bursar had its problems. "I do suppose," he wrote State Secretary and Treasurer Manly, "the business connected with this same Bursarship is of as complicated and vexatious character as is done in North Carolina. There have been paid out in this session something more than 1200 dollars. This I have to pay out, and not a little of it in tens, fives and fours . . ."

After the departure of Professor Olmsted to Yale, he took over geology as well as chemistry and mineralogy. Sometimes he took all three daughters on geologic trips, testing their knowledge (gossip said) of Greek verbs along the way. One of his first classes included the student James K. Polk, subsequently President of the United States.

In a letter to her mother back in Connecticut, Mrs. Mitchell told of being invited to dine at President Caldwell's house. "Shall I tell you of what a Carolina dinner consisted?" she wrote. "Roast turkey and duck, roast beef and boiled, broiled chicken, Irish and sweet potatos, turnips, rice, carrots, parsnips, cabbage, stewed apples, boiled pudding, baked potato puddings, damson tarts, currant tarts, apple pies, and whips."

There were no chain stores then. Just food.

The Mystery in the Benton Case

I

On March 19, 1799, Thomas Hart Benton of Hillsborough, North Carolina, who lived to become a United
States Senator, a builder of the new frontier in the West,
and a political power second only to Clay, Calhoun, Webster, and Andrew Jackson, was expelled from the Philanthropic Society, manned by University of North Carolina
students. This was tantamount to expulsion from the University, and Benton left the same day, never to return to
Chapel Hill.

The charge against him was the theft of monies from his
fellow students and roommates.

The page containing the account of the March 19 expulsion has disappeared from the Philanthropic Society
minutes.

What happened to the missing document?

Was it removed by accident or design?

As to the possibility of accident, a note attached to the
old records by an unnamed University librarian says:
"Several pages of these minutes for April, 1799, were
bound through error in Dialectic Society (rival of the Philanthropic) Minutes, Vol. 2." (The missing portion for
March 19, 1799, was lost long before this mistake—it is not
among the items in the Dialectic Minutes).

There have been numerous attempts to arrive at or to
suggest a solution of the mystery. One of the investigators

of the case was Henri Harrisse, historian and University instructor, who went into the mutilated records July 12, 1856, and wrote he had "found nothing." He added:

"There seems to be a chasm from Mar 1 to Mar 26—the records of the intervening meeting have been torn off."

In 1856, the year of Harrisse's report, Benton was living in Washington, D. C. and writing about his political battles between 1820 and 1850 in his *Thirty Years' Review*, in which he does not mention either Chapel Hill or the University. Benton, however, was a man of tremendous contradictions, and if he harbored any animosity against the University or his former literary society, he did not show it in his letter to Julian E. Sawyer, University student and member of the Philanthropic Society, dated Senate Chamber, Dec. 18, 1832:

"Dear sir, Your letter of November was duly received after my arrival at this place, and in answer to your inquiry I have the honor to state that it will give me pleasure to contribute, according to my means, to the laudable object of your Society, say about $20. Wishing you, and the young gentlemen of the Society, every prosperity, I have the honor to be yours truly, Thomas H. Benton"

This indication of Benton's goodwill no doubt influenced his reinstatement in the Society after 38 years had passed. On May 9, 1837, member G. Shepard is thus recorded:

"I move that Thomas H. Benton be readmitted as a member of our society. I further move that a certificate certifying the same signed by the president and secretary be transmitted to Mr. Benton."

No acknowledgment by Senator Benton is on record.

II

Thomas Hart Benton entered the University, then only four years old, at the age of 16 on January 1, 1798, when George Washington was President of the United States. Benton's home was on the banks of the Eno River three miles from Hillsborough, which had been the colonial capital. He had attended a school in Hillsborough operated by Richard Stanford, a New England teacher. In his parentage Benton was fortunate. His father, Jesse Benton, was a prosperous lawyer with a good library and a bent toward speculation in land. If Jesse was of a scholarly disposition, Thomas's mother, "Nancy," who was Ann Gooch of Hanover County, Virginia, was a woman of action. A few years after her husband's death she had increased the estate to a thousand acres or more and was the owner of six slaves. Early in his life she had exacted a promise from Thomas that he would abstain from tobacco, cards, and liquor. This promise he kept. It was one of his sources of strength when it was common for men to waste their substance and time in these three indulgences, for Piedmont North Carolina had a frontier psychology with its tendency toward drinking, disputes, exaggerated egos and violence.

At the time of Benton's matriculation the University had just eighty students, most of whom roomed in the two-story "East Wing" as the Old East Dormitory was then called. He was placed in a room with three other students, who were destined to have a pronounced influence on his inchoate career. Of this group the leader was William Cherry, a planter's son from Bertie County, who was graduated with a Bachelor of Arts degree in 1800 and became a lawyer, a member of the House of Commons and a University trustee. He was of a friendly disposition and showed an immediate interest in young Benton. Cherry was talented and might have gone far had he not had a weakness for the third of Nancy Benton's forbidden temptations, the bottle, which led him into dissipation and a shortened career. Another roommate was Fleming Saunders, of Rocky Mount, Va., who became a member of Virginia's General Assembly and a judge of Virginia's General Court. The third occupant was Marmaduke Baker of Gates County, North Carolina, of whom not much is known.

By the middle of April, 1798, Benton had earned an "approved" notation on a Latin examination in Virgil and two other faculty notations for "breaches of discipline." The result of one of these breaches was summed up by Thomas G. Amis, writing from Chapel Hill to Ebenezer Pettigrew in Tyrrell County, this item from news of the campus: "Thomas Benton and Benjamin Sherrod are suspended until next January." Pettigrew in reply wrote in regard to the punishment of Benton: "I suppose, however, it was not for building churches."

This is sufficient indication that the University of North Carolina campus was already aware of Benton's tendencies. He had been suspended for six months for his part in what was called the Lytle affair in the first week of April, 1798, when Archibald Lytle, a student from Tennessee, which was still a part of North Carolina, was angered by a roughing up administered to his nephew, John Lytle. Archibald publicly threatened a whipping to John's assailants. Benton came up and, according to the faculty records, "asked for the whipping promised." Benton then ran and got a horsewhip. Lytle ran and got a pistol. Benton then produced a pistol of his own. (Pistols were then a normal part of a student's baggage.) A witness at the faculty hearing testified that "Benton said he had tried his pistol and had sent a ball two inches into a hard piece of oak." Lytle put up his pistol, saying he did not wish to risk faculty punishment. Benton did not deny he had intended to shoot Lytle but meant only to hit him "under the shoulder." Dr. Joseph Caldwell, the University President, was opposed to these student confrontations with arms and no doubt influenced the faculty's verdict of six months' suspension for Benton.

On Benton's return to the campus early in 1799, he could choose membership in either of the two literary and debating societies maintained by the students: the Philanthropic, which was supposed to represent the eastern half of the long State of North Carolina, or the Dialectic, which attracted the western students. These two societies enforced strict discipline and compelled close attention to business. In an era of a frontier that disregarded rules, they gave their members a taste of orderly and democratic debate. All the rest of his life Benton exhibited the influence and ideals of these student societies.

The Philanthropic minutes of the period show that Benton's petition for membership was handed in by William Cherry, his roommate, and friend, and was at once sanctioned. In February, 1798, Benton, who was not yet 17, proposed the question for the next debate—"whether it is most conducive to public utility that the power of disposing of posts under the government should be vested in the president or legislative body." A week later he was listed as a speaker before the society, along with his roommates Baker and Cherry. Benton and Cherry were appointed "to support the effects of the French revolution." Already the rude country boy from the Eno River was having his ideas carried far beyond the boundaries of his county and was being led to think both nationally and internationally.

III

The next month could have been called the Ides of March for Benton; and what follows here is a condensation of a long and detailed faculty examination dealing with him. It began with a statement by Fleming Saunders, one of three Benton roommates, that he had asked Benton to keep his purse safely for him in Benton's trunk. When next he went into his purse, he said he had found $9 missing. Then William Cherry complained that $8 had been taken from his coat during the night. A climax came when Marmaduke Baker testified he had found his money short by $18 plus a shilling.

The three youths conferred on what to do. Cherry offered a clue by saying that in his money had been a new federal $1 note. A store clerk reported he had seen such a note in Benton's possession. The boys were now convinced that Benton's conduct was suspicious, especially his habit of staying up later than his roommates. They took their suspicions to University President Caldwell, who agreed that a trap should be set for Benton. On the night of March 16 the boys noted that Benton tied his neckerchief carefully before retiring, and on this occasion Saunders outdid Benton by staying awake later than he. At last Benton went to sleep. Saunders and the other boys then searched Benton's clothing and found, they said, Cherry's unique $1 note.

The next day the boys decoyed Benton into taking a walk in the woods with them. There they accused Benton of robbing them. Benton, they said, confessed taking their money but declared he had intended to replace it. On March 19, just after his 17th birthday, Benton was expelled from the Philanthropic Society and the University. Legend says that as he rode his horse away, he exclaimed to onlooking students, "Damn you, you will hear from me again." Whether or not he said that or something similar, he made that promise good.

His departure did not end the thieving charges. In a few days Saunders and Baker escorted to Benton's home a fourth student named Thomas King, of Sampson County, subsequently a major in the United States Army in the War of 1812 and a member of the State House of Commons. Calling Benton out of his house, King accused him of taking money from his trunk. Benton admitted having a key made and opening King's trunk.

All this testimony against Benton is contained in the University faculty records for 1799. These records do not indicate that Benton presented, or was invited to present, his case; or that he was allowed to face his accusers at the hearing. It is considered extraordinary that anyone as bellicose as Benton should have been so passive during the investigation of the thefts, and that he had nothing to say in his defense except that he had intended to replace the monies taken. Little or no palliation has been offered from his side except that his strong-willed mother had unduly limited his spending money. Most of the several biographies on Benton have either ignored or muffled the charges against him at Chapel Hill, and even so voluminous and candid a historian as Dr. Kemp P. Battle, post-Civil War President of the University and its professor of history, makes only a vague reference to the Benton case, and that without mentioning his name, in his history of the University in the following lines (Vol. I, p. 194):

"As to the charge of theft brought against one who afterwards became famous in the councils of the nation, I conclude that it arose from a mistake, distorted by the fierce party spirit of the day."

However, William Nisbet Chambers, author of *Old Bullion Benton, Senator from the New West,* writes this in the 1956 edition, page 16: "There can be little doubt that Thomas did steal the money, for though his roommates may have disliked him and the Faculty Records contain only their testimony and that of one other student, to put the whole thing down as a hoax requires too many improbable assumptions and too much credulity in general."

Whatever may be the ultimate truth about Benton's expulsion from the Philanthropic Society and the disappearance from the minutes of the decision in his case, it is a fact that he and his widowed mother (his father died in the winter of 1790-91) accepted the verdict with remarkable quietude considering his aggressive disposition and her similar temperament. For two years after his departure from Chapel Hill he remained at home, probably reading copiously in his father's well-stocked library and practicing with firearms for recreation. His mother had meantime moved her family across the Eno to a 215-acre farm at Hart's Mill, also called Hartford, a rural establishment which had belonged to an uncle and which had figured in the Revolutionary War so recently ended. Later events indicated that Benton, no doubt swayed by his debating experience in the Philanthropic Society, had already decided that his profession was to be the practice of law.

IV

At the end of this period Benton's mother gathered up
her eight children, her slaves and belongings, and moved to
the Cumberland River Valley in Tennessee, which was still
a part of North Carolina. In her husband's lifetime he had
been rated as the largest landowner in this region, claiming
30,000 acres. She settled down on a homestead claim of 2,560
acres on Leiper's Fork of the West Harpeth River, 25
miles south of Nashville. Here a community grew up that
became known as Benton Town, then as Hillsborough, no
doubt recalling the old North Carolina home. Thomas assisted on the farm, then for a time taught school, but before
reaching his majority he pushed both occupations aside and
went for the law. He was now a bulky and muscular figure,
loving oratory and florid writing, and a keen student of
men and their habits.

In 1806 he obtained his law license and at once entered
local politics, preaching reform of the courts, cheap land
for settlers, and whatever would benefit farmers and small
traders. At the age of 27 he was elected to the Tennessee
Senate and began the political career which carried him
high, though never as high as he would have liked. In
1812 he was appointed a colonel of army volunteers.

Three years later he was convinced he needed a wider
field and moved to St. Louis, a frontier town of some 5,000
people, where there was abundant practice in land entries,
land claims, land quarrels, and land lawsuits. He became involved in a quarrel with a young man named Charles Lucas.
At that time and place men talked much of their "honor" as
if it were a delicate plant not to be brushed against, much
less trodden upon. Benton called Lucas a puppy. Lucas

challenged him to a duel. Benton obliged and killed him. Bleeding to death, Lucas forgave him. The episode caused Benton such horror that he burned all the records pertaining to the case and never welcomed any reference to it. But he remained locked to his career and a year later took a step that would make him a power in Missouri politics: he acquired in 1818 a newspaper and named it the St. Louis *Enquirer*. With this he was able to belabor land frauds and other commercial dealings besides the uncertainty and flimsiness of paper money, which he demanded should be replaced by a reliable gold and silver standard; hence his nickname of "Old Bullion."

Meantime he shouted for statehood. In 1820 this was granted, and Missouri became a powerful slave-holding state. With it Benton, who was no admirer of slavery, became a national figure. Even if he had had no other auxiliaries, his friendship with Andrew Jackson would have given him substantial political influence. This friendship had begun in a fracas between the two men and developed into a political intimacy that was valuable to both.

In his recollections, written when he was a Senator at Washington, Benton wrote: "The first time I saw Gen. Jackson was at Nashville, Tenn., in 1799—he on the bench, a judge of the then Superior Court, and I a youth of 17, back in the crowd." Benton added this pen portrait of Jackson: "Cordial and graceful manners, hospitable temper, clever of mind, undaunted spirit, generosity and perfect integrity."

Hardly second to Benton's devotion to Jackson was his reverence for the teachings of Thomas Jefferson. Jefferson taught that farmers were the chosen people of God, and Benton willingly accepted that as a principle. In fact, as he grew older he became so ardent a Jeffersonian that a writer once remarked that Benton "sprinkled holy water on every issue from slavery to salt."[1]

One day in 1830 Benton arranged a celebration of Jefferson's birthday as a "recurrence to fundamental principles, and a declaration of adhesion to the republican doctrines of the great apostle of American liberty." In 1820, the year of Missouri's admission to the Union, the state's capital was named Jefferson, and today 18 Missouri townships bear the name of Jefferson. In such things Benton's hand is clearly visible.

Benton in 1815 met Elizabeth McDowell, daughter of Col. James McDowell of Cherry Grove, a farm near Lexington, Virginia, and besought her to marry him. But she would not. After six years of ardent courtship by him she changed her mind and became his gentle and devoted wife and the mother of his six children. Of these, four were girls. One, Jessie Ann, married Gen. John C. Frémont, the explorer, whose candidacy for the presidency later led to the expulsion of a University of North Carolina professor for his opinions. (See chapter on "The House Shaped Like a Hexagon.")

However aggressive Benton may have been in his political pursuits, all accounts agree that his family life was quiet and affectionate. This is verified by Jessie Benton Frémont when in her book, *Souvenirs of My Time*, all her references to her father were admiring. Of her home life in Washington, she wrote:

"Our house had been bought by my father from a Boston gentleman who had lived much in London, and who built it with thick walls and spacious rooms, and beautified the

[1] Merrill D. Peterson in *The Jefferson Image in the American Mind*.

ground in the rear . . . My father believed in working while he worked, and resting completely when at rest. His library on the floor above was his working place. . . . We four sisters adapted the great square dining table for our shaded lamp, our work baskets and portfolios, and there our little world revolved."

During his years in St. Louis and Washington Benton took part in the fiercest political battles of the period. In most of them he was a leader and spokesman, and the more ferocious the battles became, the more he enjoyed them, finding that men give no quarter when their political disputes have an economic base. Included in the violent questions of the day were slavery, statehood, tariffs, currency, banking, and the admission of Texas and Oregon.

On the approach of the 1856 presidential election Benton refused to be a candidate because "all statesmanship (had been) reduced to a hurrah on one side or the other of slavery." The Republican Party's nominee was Benton's son-in-law, Gen. John C. Frémont, but Benton refused to support him because Frémont was deemed too friendly to slave owners. Benton's candidate was James Buchanan, who was elected President on a platform of peace and union.[2]

At age 74 Benton was called a "man of iron" because of his strong frame, robust health and continuous activity.

---

[2] 1856 was the year in which W. W. Holden, the secessionist editor of the Raleigh *Standard*, who later went over to the Northern forces and became the Federal Governor of North Carolina, published the anti-Frémont editorial that led to the ousting of Prof. B. S. Hedrick from the University of North Carolina because he was opposed to the extension of slavery. Holden wrote: "That man is neither a fit nor a safe instructor of our young men who even inclines to Frémont and black Republicanism."

President Buchanan visited Chapel Hill in 1859. He made a good impression by his affable manners. A newspaper correspondent wrote: "He has a kind word for every one who approaches him, and a hearty kiss for every pretty girl who has one for him."

But in 1856 he suffered his first prolonged spell of ill health and spent much time in bed. He kept up his writings but at length had to resort to whispered dictation.

By 1858 Benton's illness was recognized as terminal and he made his will and borrowed money to pay his debts. President Buchanan came to visit him, and they conversed in a friendly spirit. On April 9, 1858, Benton told his children gathered around his bedside: "I am comfortable and happy." He died early the next morning. Two days later his little grandson, McDowell Jones, also died and was buried by the side of his grandfather in Bellefontaine Cemetery, St. Louis, after a funeral procession watched by many thousands.

The Washington *Union* ascribed to Benton "gigantic intellect, strong physical constitution, and imposing presence." Historians of the period agree with these attributes except the first one, on which their verdicts are divided. Benton attained his political power and founded his career on his efforts to save the farmer, land owner, trapper and hunter from the dominance of banks and rising industry. Commercialism was becoming strong and eventually won.

The mystery surrounding Benton's departure from Chapel Hill has never been cleared away. Did he secretly remove the page of the Philanthropic Society minutes which recorded his expulsion, or did some friend or agent act for him? He was fortunate in that his Western career was not marred by his misfortunes in North Carolina. His political opponents rarely referred to the scandals of his youth. It seems to have been commonly agreed that he had well nigh erased his misdeeds by his labors for the common man.

President Caldwell, Fleet of Foot

I

On the north side of Chapel Hill is an elevated residential hill known as Mount Bolus. This is a contraction for *diabolus*, the Latin word for devil, which his students chose to apply to Dr. Joseph Caldwell, first President of the University of North Carolina.

Dr. Caldwell was not a man of surpassing stern or relentless nature. *Diabolus* was the name for him because in the cause of law and order he was wont to stroll about the campus in the dark of the night and if he encountered any mischief he at once gave chase. Being nimble of foot and not fleshy, he was capable of running malefactors down and bringing them in by the scruff of the neck. Students partaking of drink or disorderly sports, of storing cows in classrooms, of undue ringing of the campus bell after midnight, or any other forbidden activity, were liable to quick apprehension and punishment.

In Dr. Caldwell's day caning or some other form of corporal punishment for misdeeds was not unknown. It was mostly applied, to be sure, in the preparatory or "nursery" department maintained in the "east wing," as Old East Building was called, but it was not withheld from older and rawer students in certain cases. And Dr. Caldwell was the man to use it. He did not thus lose the respect of his students. They knew he was a fair-minded scholar and man who aimed at justice.

Although a scholar by nature, Dr. Caldwell was quite

proud of his sinewy physique and liked to describe his nocturnal encounters with rowdy students. One night when making his rounds he was going through a hall in South Building when he came face to face with a student who exclaimed:

"Ah, old fellow, I think I scuffled with you once before and you gave me a hard fall. I won't let you off now. Come on, I'll throw you."

Forthwith President and student wrestled with all their muscle, and the doctor was being hard pressed when luckily another student appeared with a light and brought the match to an end.

Another story which Dr. Caldwell told with great enjoyment related to the theft of his carriage by students, who took it to the edge of a swamp two miles from the campus and left it there. The doctor directed his coachman, "Dr." November, to go fetch it back the next night. The students heard of this errand and beat November to the spot. They hauled the carriage deep into the swamp, laughing meantime and mimicking a supposed conversation between the President and his servant, without being aware that Dr. Caldwell himself was seated in the carriage with the curtains drawn. The students had just paused to puff and blow when Dr. Caldwell leaned out and said:

"Well, young gentlemen, I've had a very pleasant ride. Now take me back home."

The students sheepishly did so and hauled the carriage and Dr. Caldwell back to the carriage house, where the doctor thanked them again for a pleasant ride and said good night.

Prof. William Hooper, long a teacher of ancient and modern languages at the University and builder of the house on the southeast corner of Franklin Street and Battle Lane, described the hazards and hardships of those early days in a commencement address June 1, 1859 called *Fifty Years Since*. He first arrived in Chapel Hill in January, 1804. He was then 12 years old. The infant University was practically half that age, for although it was opened to students in 1795 it was three years before its courses were well organized.

The faculty consisted of three men—Dr. Caldwell, Prof. William Bingham, and tutor Richard Henderson. They were known respectively as Old Joe, Old Slick and Little Dick. Only one dormitory had a roof. The only finished buildings were the East Wing and Old Chapel (Person Hall). The former was two stories high and housed sixty students, four in a room. South Building, only a story and a half high, was in a pathetic condition and remained unfinished for many years. The University then had an income of $15,000 a year. South Building so weighed on the President's mind that in 1811 he went on the road soliciting funds and brought in $10,000 with which work was renewed.

The model by which the University shaped itself was Princeton College, which then dominated the embryo Ivy League through its theological seminary as mother of a host of young Presbyterian preachers. In accordance with the sparse comforts permitted in that day, the students at Chapel Hill rose before daybreak and went to compulsory prayer by candlelight.

The University Library consisted of two parts, the Di and Phi collection of books contributed by members of the two literary societies, "a few half worn volumes migrated from room to room," said Professor Hooper, and were housed in one of the cupboards of the common room of Old East. The cupboards were full of rat holes, but such was the rivalry between the societies that when one installed a new book, the other must install the equivalent. The rancor of competition often led to the verge of blows. No halls were set aside for the societies' use. When they met it was in the Old Chapel that had no heat in winter and nothing to prevent the wind whistling through.

The students subsisted on the lean fare provided at Stewards Hall, a rough wooden building situated between what was later the Carr Building and the Playmakers' Theatre. Board cost $35 a year and if any student craved such luxuries as chicken dinners he could find them in the village at 25 cents a meal. These were only for the well-to-do. The poor students, filled with a rasping hunger, had to forage for the extras not afforded by Stewards Hall and any house in the village or garden with a larder not well guarded was liable to find missing anything eatable.

Stewards Hall was occasionally the scene of balls and other social diversions such as fights. One of these took place between Hyder Ali Davie, son of General Davie (who named him for an Oriental enemy of Great Britain) and Henry Chambers of Salisbury. Young Davie was accused of stabbing his adversary and was reprimanded by the trustees.

Major Pleasant Henderson, who managed Stewards Hall, resented aspersions on his bills of fare and particularly objected to a report by a Committee of Visitation which declared that "his invariable service of mutton and of bacon too fat to be eaten and nearly starved the boys." The major said with feeling, "This report comes like a thunderclap on me, because I knew it was founded on information false as hell." Moreover, his emotions were so violent that "appearances are indication of, if not ruin, the most severe stroke I ever had."

II

Dr. Caldwell found life hard without the refinements to which he had been accustomed and more than once tried to resign and go back to New Jersey, where his birthplace was Leamington. His father was a physician, belonging to a Scotch-Irish family. His mother was Rachel Harker, daughter of a Presbyterian minister. The UNC President was graduated from Princeton College, the former College of New Jersey, in 1791 at the age of 19 and was later licensed to preach. He was a teacher of mathematics at Princeton when called to take the chair of mathematics tutor at Chapel Hill at $600 a year. He was then only 23 years old.

Dr. Charles W. Harris, then faculty chairman, advised him not to undergo the expense and tedium of a journey down by boat and coach, but to buy a horse, "small but good," and hitch it to a "chair," which was a sort of two-wheel sulky seating one person. Linen, stockings, shoes, broadcloth and other clothing could be stored in a trunk and shipped to Petersburg, whence it would be taken to Hillsborough. The young teacher took this advice and drove down alone by way of Washington, Alexandria, Richmond, and Petersburg, arriving at Chapel Hill safely October 31, 1796. He left no notes about his adventures on the way down and made only one recorded comment about his impressions after arriving.

"The State," he wrote, "appears to be swarming with lawyers." He also remarked: "Religion is little in vogue." In fact, there had been an ebbtide in religious belief in both America and Europe, culminating in the extreme opinions and actions of the French Revolution, and this backwash had been felt throughout the thirteen colonies.

Dr. Caldwell, soon after his arrival, wanted to resign. In the Chapel Hill of his day he found little or no intellectual companionship and an absence of religious sentiment. The University had been laid down at a crossroads in the midst of endless forests. The land had been contributed by hard-working farmers who, having had small schooling, were all the more anxious that their sons should be college-bred. The students who first matriculated at the University were mostly of a frontier spirit, believing in violent amusements, and privately owned more pistols than books.

All this was alien to the tastes and upbringing of Dr. Caldwell, and he probably would have insisted on his resignation had he not received constant encouragement from Gen. W. R. Davie, Father of the University in more than one sense. It is on record that he spent two successive evenings with Dr. Caldwell, no doubt giving to the doctor the benefit of his experiences not only with Chapel Hill but the State of North Carolina.

"The more I know Caldwell the more I am pleased with him," said the General, and that verdict kept the doctor in Chapel Hill for the rest of his life. But he was chairman of the faculty only. It was 1808 before he was made President.

However, in 1812 he resigned and occupied the chair of mathematics for five years. His successor was Dr. Robert Chapman, who did not please the trustees, and in 1816 Dr. Caldwell by request resumed the presidency. Seven years later the tide of interest in science felt in Europe and eastern America in the late 18th century, reached North Carolina and Dr. Caldwell was encouraged by the trustees to go to Europe to seek "philosophical apparatus" and books for an enlarged library. During his absence of ten months he visited England, Scotland, France, Switzerland, and Germany. To one of his temperament this journey must have been thrilling, yet he left not a word of written comment about it. Instead, after his return, signing himself "Carlton," he wrote a laborious series of articles for the State newspapers urging more internal improvements in North Carolina, particularly a railroad from Beaufort to the mountains. The State paid no attention.

However, his scientific investigation in Europe did bear some fruit. He brought back a marked interest in astronomy and mounted a telescope on the roof of his house, which stood approximately where the President's house now stands, and he also erected in the rear of his backyard garden two "meridian pillars" pointing to the north. These pillars still stand in a little court of their own in the rear of the President's house, having been restored by Prof. James Lee Love of U.N.C. and Harvard University. An inscription between them reads:

> Meridian pillars built by Joseph Caldwell, President of the University of NC 1804-1812. 1816-1835, shortly after his return in 1824 for the procurement of astronomical instruments and books.

Dr. Caldwell was twice married. His first wife was Susan Rowan of Fayetteville, who died after only three years of marriage. His second was Helen Hooper, the widow of William Hooper, son of the Signer, who is buried in Hillsborough. She was the daughter of James Hogg, a Scots merchant of Hillsborough. She lies beside her husband under the white shaft in the middle of the campus grove of oaks. "She was a woman to take the lead and keep it," wrote Cornelia Phillips Spencer. She also wrote this description of Dr. Caldwell: "Middle height, eyes dark and penetrating, bushy eyebrows, clothing neat, precise and handsome." She believed him to be the last man in Chapel Hill who attended balls in 18th century costume—knee breeches, silk stockings, and silver buckle shoes. She also described him as taking a jug of liquor to the field hands working at a clearing—a sign that the puritanic culture of the times was not prohibitionist.

Dr. Caldwell's later years were afflicted by a painful disease, and he had to have the administrative help of Adjunct Professor Walker Anderson, who always said the doctor owed much of his talents and character to his Huguenot grandmother, Rachel Lovel. In politics Dr. Caldwell was a Federalist and had no sympathy with the teachings of Thomas Jefferson, against whom there was a severe reaction in the 1830's. The University's first President died in 1835 after 31 years of residence in Chapel Hill.

The Two Oldest Buildings on the Campus

I

Old East Building on the campus of the University is the oldest state university building in the country. It dates back to the administration of George Washington. It has several other distinctions. It has been repaired and added to more often than any other campus structure, and its chief parent, so to speak, was the Father of the University, Gen. W. R. Davie, who was continually at war with the original contractor, James Patterson. The building is not only the oldest of its kind in Chapel Hill but it was probably the cheapest. Its original cost was put at $5,000.

The University's charter is dated 1789, but it was 1793 before Old East was begun. It was completed as designed in 1795, two stories high. It was the first University building to be adequately sketched by one of its occupants, John Pettigrew, who sent the sketch home to his father, the Bishop of Edenton, in 1797.

When the cornerstone was laid in 1793 it was supposed to contain a plate recording the date, October 12, now annually observed as University Day, and other details. This plate was found 123 years later in Tennessee in a scrap pile bought by a foundry. Luckily the owner was a University alumnus, Thomas B. Foust, Class of 1903, who recognized its value and returned it to the University, where it is preserved in the Wilson Library. How this plate got out of Chapel Hill into Clarksville, Tenn., and was lost for more than a century, has never been adequately explained. It was engraved by Roswell Huntington, who came to Hillsborough from Connecticut in 1786 and set up as a silversmith.

The warfare between General Davie and Patterson, the contractor, reached a climax as Old East neared completion. The general relieved his ire by a letter dated July 23, 1795, to the State Treasurer, John Haywood. "Patterson became extremely clamorous," wrote Davie, "to be paid for his extra work. The Board [of Trustees], being pressed on this head, took it up; but his charges were found so excessively exorbitant and his work so infamously done, that they referred it again to the Commissioners. I verily believe he has charged six or seven prices for the painting, the rest of the work is on the same ratio." A year later Davie was still denouncing Patterson for "endless vexation."[1]

Patterson replied with moans of grief and self pity. "I have been a very Considerable Sufferer by the contract," he wrote, "having not only sank (*sic*) several hundreds of pounds but also nearly two years hard service without benefiting one farthing by it."

Patterson also wrote to State Treasurer Haywood with injured feelings and irregular spelling, saying: "When I undertook this building I thought I Had to do with a Set gentlemen that would not Quibble about triffles (*sic*); and I should be sorry to say I have Reason to think so now. In the first place I have been Severely Handled by ill Grounded suspitions (*sic*) that I would not finish the building undertaken.

"Secondly, brick delayed two months.

"Thirdly, second payment delayed three months.

"Last payment not met—not only hurts my credit by my

[1] Robinson, *William R. Davie.*

feelings." He mentioned that a writ had been served on him about a village lot and for balance due on a sawmill.

This reference to a lot probably indicates the one of two acres bought by Patterson at the 1793 sale in Chapel Hill. He lived in an old house used as an inn on the southwest corner of Franklin and Columbia Streets which he sold in 1795 to William and Elizabeth Nunn, who conducted a famous "house of entertainment" there for several years. As for the delays in payment of which Patterson complained, the accounts of Walter Alves, University Treasurer, show these amounts paid to Patterson in 1795:

> Feb. 7   £300
> April 17 £533-6-8
> Aug. 15   £170
> Sept. 14 £113-7-4

The commissioners who awarded the contract for Old East to Patterson were W. R. Davie, Alfred Moore, Frederick Hargett, Thomas Blount, Alexander Mebane, John Williams and John Haywood. It called for a building 96 feet seven inches long, 40 feet one inch wide, two stories high, to contain 16 rooms, and four passageways for 50 students; eight rooms on a floor with a chimney to each room; a closet in each room with six shelves fixed in the plaster; a plain chimney piece over each fireplace; the roof strong, not heavy, but well framed and braced; the whole of the brick work to be laid in mortar made of lime and sand, with pine shingles; the whole to be done and executed in "a plain but neat, substantial and workmanlike manner." The foundation was to have a bottom wall of stone three feet thick. The commissioners contracted for 350,000 bricks at £140.

Gen. Davie's complaint about Patterson's high prices for painting is partly verified by the latter's bill in 1793:

> "13 jugs of Lintseedoile (*sic*) imported at 50/, £32-10-0
> 1 keg of imported yallow-oaker in oile £ 3-15-0
> Part of a keg of Spanish brown in oile £ 2-10-0
> 10 cwt of dry yallow-oaker, 8 ditto £ 3-6-8

> "Total £123-16-8
> To cartage,
> grinding,
> mixing, and
> painting £123-16-8
>   £247-16-8"

Patterson's charge of more than £32 for 13 jugs of linseed oil and his doubling of the total by charges for cartage, etc., were well calculated to arouse General Davie's suspicion and ire.

Old East was originally called the North Wing. The campus was designed to be a square, running east to the west line of the K. P. Battle lot, and west to the east line of Swain Hall; from Cameron Avenue 21° west to Franklin Street and south to the Raleigh Road, west of the Bell Tower, all in terms of modern nomenclature. The central plan called for two wide strips of land at right angles, to be called "avenues," one running north 21° west, the other north 69° east. The north strip was called Grand Avenue. Where it crossed the present Franklin Street it was 240 feet wide (Battle's History says 290 feet), representing extensions of the east wall of Old East and the west wall of Old West dormitories. An avenue not named was to be 150 feet wide running from the present South Building site to Piney Prospect. In the pre-Civil War Swain administration it was decided, in order to raise funds, to sell off the north strip in tracts. Grand Avenue, which was supposed to run down to Bolin's Creek, was broken by the insertion of a union church and lot which were sold about 1849 to the Presbyterian Church. On this tract the church buildings rest today.

In a 1793 note General Davie wrote: "The town consists of one principal street laid off in lots of two acres each, parallel with the north front of the buildings. There are also six lots of four acres each, located on the most elegant situations contiguous to the University." It was doubtless one of these two-acre lots that Patterson bought and was unable to pay for until he got his contract money.

In 1844 General Davie's denunciations of Patterson seemed justified. Neither Old East nor its companion, Old West, were deemed adequate, and A. J. Davis, the New York architect who did much to give the homely campus buildings the style which they lacked, was engaged to draw plans to enlarge both Old East and Old West one half their length northward for $9,360. Davis added to Old East a third floor and gave its north face some distinction by adding a columnar effect with recessed vertical frames or pillars. The same treatment was given to Old West. The effect was dignified and stately, although there was little ground for Chapel Hill's belief that it was very exotic and Egyptian.

Old East staggered along, so to speak, until 1922 when its condition drew examiners who found renovation impracticable and suggested the building be junked. They pointed to a bulge in the brick walls, resulting from interior pressure. This was relieved by a concrete framework inside. At the same time the east side porticos were restored, imparting further dignity to what had been called "a huge misshapen pile." The cost of repairing both Old East and Old West at this time, 1925, was $127,000.

With these repairs Old East "made out," as it were, until 1948 when it was partly remodeled and its interior fireproofed. Minor repairs have continued at intervals ever since. Age and its peculiar tint, ranging from light yellow to a red clay color, have given Old East an authoritative and almost sacred position on the University campus.

II

Second to Old East in age is Person Hall, named for its chief donor, Gen. Thomas Person of Granville County, known in his day as "the Old Regulator." It has another distinction: it is the only campus building that has arched, not rectangular, windows.

The University was only a year or two old when it was agreed that the students and faculty must have a chapel for religious services and something like an auditorium to be used for public lectures and meetings. The site was chosen to front on Grand Avenue, and digging for the foundation was begun when an old drawback to University procedure was discovered—lack of money. General Person, who was a plantation owner in what is now Warren County, came to the rescue with a gift of $1,050. Legend says the sum was paid all in one lump with shining silver dollars.

The superintendent of construction was Samuel Hopkins, who, General Davie wrote, "is almost as bad as Patterson," the builder of Old East. Work crept along slowly. Joseph Caldwell, the new President, coming down from Princeton in 1796, could descry only "the foundation of a chapel . . . the completion is uncertain, as the mason and his Negroes have spent the favorable fall in raising the foundation to the surface of the ground."

What we now know as Person Hall consists of three sections, the central one running east and west, and two wings placed at right angles. What was then called "the old chapel," although it was relatively in its infancy, was the east wing only. It measured 36 by 54 feet, built by the contractor, Philemon Hodges, of one story brick for $2,826. It endured as "the old chapel" for 40 years, used for all meetings of a public character and for sunrise prayers which all students were required to attend. Mrs. Cornelia Phillips Spencer called it headquarters for "all itinerant preachers, lecturers, showmen, ventriloquists, Siamese twins, and the like." Her mother, Judith Phillips, the wife of Prof. James Phillips, taught Sunday School there for several years up to about 1830. In 1824 Prof. Elisha Mitchell, newly arrived from Connecticut, saw it as "not a splendid but a very neat edifice."

What was probably the first University commencement was held in Person Hall in July, 1798, and succeeding commencements took place there until 1837 when the exercises were moved to Gerrard Hall. Meantime the University continued to hand out diplomas bearing the inscription *Aula Personica*, although it had been abandoned for graduation purposes for nearly 40 years.

After 1875 Person Hall was used as a reading room and was then assigned to Physics and Chemistry, next to Medicine, then in turn to Pharmacy, to the University Press, Music, and the Playmakers. Thus it passed from hand to hand until 1933 when the trustees, noting a current setting in toward the arts, voted to make the Hall a fine arts building. The east wing became a workshop, the center, built in

1886, an art gallery with walls suitable for display, and the west wing a smaller gallery with a library and offices attached. The west wing was built for $2,645 out of a fund of $13,000 given to the University by Miss Mary Ann Smith for a chair of agricultural chemistry.

General Person was never adequately thanked for his donation. In 1810 the University trustees passed a resolution that there should be set into the wall of the Hall "a neat marble slab, surmounted by an urn or some ornament of that kind" to cost £40-50 as an acknowledgment of his gift. This resolution was never carried out.

General Person was one of the founding fathers of the University but somehow his life and career have never received the study they deserve. He was a radical when most of his associates were conservative and aristocratic; he was a democrat when his ownership of 67,437 acres of land should have made him property conscious; he was sympathetic toward the Regulators when the colonial government considered them reptiles; and he was for American independence when the British government still had a strong following in North Carolina.

He began life as a surveyor for Lord Granville, but after the Hillsborough riot of oppressed farmers in 1770 he was put on Governor Tryon's suspect list. According to legend, he was rescued from Tryon's clutches by the Rev. George Micklejohn, who remained royalist long after his congregations had turned rebel. Person in gratitude gave the clergyman a house called "The Glade" on the plantation named Goshen. Person joined the Provincial Council in 1776 and was on the Halifax committee which on April 12, 1776, passed a resolution urging independence. He was a member of the General Assembly for 16 years, helped to frame the University charter, and was on its first board of trustees.

It was in the years following the Revolutionary War that General Person showed his basic sentiments, and in a sense Person Hall stands as a monument to, or a reminder of, a tremendous crisis in North Carolina history. This came in the fiery debate over the United States Constitution. North Carolina opposed it unless it had drastic amendments in a fight led by Willie (pronounced Wylie) Jones, the State's foremost liberal. He was strongly supported by Person. Jones and Person were for local self-government, states' rights, and wide civil liberties. They feared standing armies, judges as rulers, and high taxation. Opposed to them was General Davie, the University's Father, who was an ardent Federalist and strict conservative, as was most of the University community. He accused Person of taking "much pain out of doors to irritate the minds of his countrymen against the Constitution." If so, Person was successful, for the Hillsborough constitutional convention of 1788 rejected the proposed Constitution by 184 votes to 84. Thus for a time North Carolina was a foreign and independent government. The broadened document, with far stronger guarantees for individual liberties and a clear bill of rights, passed at Fayetteville in 1789. At this same Fayetteville convention Davie introduced his bill to establish the University of North Carolina. Thus it can be said that Person Hall is a monument to the preservation of liberties that we know today. It also signalized the first step taken toward higher education in this State.

Those persons acquainted with the political battles of this period can, as they pass and look upon sturdy Person Hall, reflect that the man for whom it is named was in some measure responsible for the fact that we enjoy today the basic rights of speech and press, assembly, petition and religion as contained in the amendments to the United States Constitution. Although a great landowner and slave holder, General Person was like Thomas Jefferson, a champion of the small farmer and little man everywhere, but particularly in Piedmont and Western North Carolina. It was in the eastern third of the State that the planters, merchants and lawyers enjoyed political as well as economic dominance. Their leader was General Davie, whose name is no less attached to Old East Building than General Person's name is to Person Hall.

"The Temple of Folly"

"A palace-like erection, which is much too large for usefulness, and might be aptly termed the 'Temple of Folly' planned by the Demi-God Davie."

Thus did an early newspaper critic signing himself "Citizen" refer to South Building, the cornerstone of which was laid on April 14, 1798.

South Building, the creamy three-story structure which once housed the chief administrative offices and lies between the North and South quadrangles, appears to us to have very simple, plain, and harmonious lines. It is devoid of ornament or "gingerbread" work. Yet the University archives show that it was bitterly criticized by those persons who saw Gen. William R. Davie, "Father of the University," and the first faculty members as upholders of Federalist if not monarchical principles; and they made the task of completing this central building a laborious and halting one.

As so often happened in the case of important university buildings, there wasn't enough money to complete it properly, and after its walls had been built up a story and a half high, it remained roofless for years.

Dr. K. P. Battle writes in his story of the University that about 1830 under the influence of Dr. Elisha Mitchell, an attempt was made to have the building face south instead of north, in keeping with its smaller neighbor, Gerrard Hall, which once had a porch on its south side. Possibly it was at this time that the name "Main" gave way to "South."

This south-looking tendency was encouraged a few years

ago when South Building was restored and improved, and ever since then the students have loved to gather happily on the south side steps during morning intermissions in winter, sun themselves there on crisp days, sip drinks from the nearby "Y" fountain, and carry on boy-meets-girl colloquies.

In 1801 the University, having failed to raise the money for South Building otherwise, decided to raise it by a lottery, and a circular of the next year says, "the interests of the University of North Carolina and of learning and of science generally, are concerned in the immediate sale of these tickets." The top prize was $1,500, the lowest $5. The net profit obtained by the University was $2,215.45. Then a second lottery was held, bringing in $2,865.36, making a total of just over $5,000 procured from the two lotteries.

This was not enough, and in 1809 and again in 1811 Dr. Joseph Caldwell, President of the University, was compelled to climb into his "stick-back-gig" and travel over the State, soliciting funds in person.

Eventually he raised about $12,000, and with this fund the building was completed and the students were able to move into the rooms set aside for them. Previously they had improvised living quarters for themselves in the roofless structure by building shacks and cabins in the corners. Dr. William Hooper, grandson of the signer of the Declaration of Independence, in his *Fifty Years Since* says the students had done this to escape the crowded conditions in the East Building, where they were herded four to a room. He adds: "As soon as Spring brought back the swallows and the leaves, they emerged from this den and chose some shady retirement, where they made a path and a promenade"—doubtless back of the South Building where numerous paths once wandered through the hardwood groves and where there was more than one spring.

Dr. Hooper imparts another curious fact, that holidays at this time were sometimes given, owing to inclement weather, which "prevented study."

South Building for years housed the chief literary societies, the Dialectic and Philanthropic, and some of the leading professors had classrooms in it. Into these latter rooms students sometimes overnight laboriously hauled cows and other cattle, ready to astonish the professors on opening next morning. They also carried cows into the belfry and set up vehicles on the roof, enjoying the sight of janitors removing them the next day.

Where They Danced

"At commencement ball, when I graduated, 1818," General E. J. Mallett, alumnus of the University, once wrote, "my coat was broadcloth of sea-green color, high velvet collar to match, swallow-tail, pockets outside with lapels, and large silver-plated buttons; white satin damask vest, showing the edge of a blue undervest; a wide opening for bosom ruffles, and no shirt collar. The neck was dressed with a layer of four or five three-cornered cravats, artistically laid, and surmounted with a cambric stock, pleated and buckled behind. My pantaloons were white canton crape, lined with pink muslin, and showed a peach-blossom tint. They were rather short, in order to display flesh-colored silk stockings, and this exposure was increased by very low-cut pumps with shiny buckles. My hair was very black, very long and queued."

This ball was probably held at Mrs. Nunn's, which was the first village hotel (it stood at the southwest corner of Franklin and Columbia Streets), but thirty-years later it might have been given in what is now called the Playmakers' Theatre, which was formerly known as Smith Hall. This building once housed the University Library, but previous to that it was the favorite hall for balls and dances. It was named for Gen. Benjamin Smith of Brunswick, N. C., a Revolutionary War officer, who fought under Moultrie in South Carolina. He was several times elected to the North Carolina General Assembly and in 1810 became Governor of the State.

His was the first donation to higher education in North Carolina, consisting of warrants for 20,000 acres of Tennessee

land awarded to him for his services in the Revolutionary
War. These he gave to the University as one of its first
trustees. The land ultimately sold for $14,000, out of which
fund Smith Hall was erected in 1850. The architect was
A. J. Davis of New York, who was under the influence of
the Greek Revival and Palladian designs which so impressed
Thomas Jefferson when he first went to Europe as envoy
to France. The builder was Capt. John Berry, State Senator.
The building has the gracious and simple lines, also the
pillared porch, of celebrated Greek temples. A novel and
regional touch was given to the front columns. The capitals
bear, instead of the lotus and acanthus leaves characteristic
of Mediterranean decorations, the corn and wheat that
spring from nearby native soil.

Governor Smith's end was a sad one. His body was seized
by creditors, who prevented burial until their demands were
satisfied. Besides this charming Greek building, one other
noteworthy and controversial object in this State bears his
name—Smith Island, also called Baldhead, lying off South-
port (once called Smithville) at the mouth of the Cape Fear.
This island has semi-tropical flora and fauna.

Before the Civil War the chief commencement dances
given in Smith Hall were always known as balls, and the
ball managers were among the most important of students;
but after the war, balls began to be called "Germans," led
by gentlemen who could carry out elaborate cotillion figures.

These dances became the target of pleasure-opposing
elements in the population, who criticized Chapel Hill as
being a "center of aristocracy." They bitterly attacked the
University authorities for permitting such dances to take
place. Nevertheless, the dances went on, as they always will
where young people gather. President Kemp P. Battle, after

reopening of the University in 1875, would never interfere with them; and gradually commencement dances at Chapel Hill regained their prestige and color. The young ladies who came to attend them—driving up Franklin Street in open barouches—gave a thrill to all beholders and their names and costumes occupied columns in the State papers.

Smith Hall had one other use. Just below it, partly covered now by Steele Dormitory, Saunders Hall, and Bynum Hall, lay the University's first large athletic field, and here, on the porch, on the steps leading to it, and on the turfy banks of the south side, the youth and fashion of Chapel Hill used to gather of late afternoons to watch the strange games of baseball and football played by young men who sometimes wore handle-bar mustaches and hair that fell into their eyes.

Spiders, Novels and Jealousy

I

Nicholas Marcellin Hentz came to Chapel Hill in 1826 as professor of the French Language and Literature, but made a name for himself as a collector of and writer on spiders. He became the leading arachnologist of his time.

Caroline Lee Hentz came with him as wife and mother, but made a name for herself as a novelist, playwright, and story writer.

No stranger couple ever lived in Chapel Hill. Outwardly Hentz was a mild and unworldly scientist; inwardly he was a barely suppressed volcano of unrest, suspicion and jealousy. His jealousy, which at times flared into a frenzy, was not concerned with other scientists but with his talented and charming wife, who never gave him any genuine cause for violent emotions. His son Charles, who was born in Chapel Hill in 1827, wrote of him:

"He was of a very affectionate, kind disposition, but at the same time one of the most nervous, jealous, suspicious characters that ever lived."[1] Hentz consisted of two warring halves and never knew peace. Nor did his patient young wife who had in the words of her son Charles, "one of the most lovely sunny dispositions that ever existed, was charming in person and conversation, and was always a center of attraction wherever she went."[2]

Dr. Hentz records other habits of his eccentric father.

[1] *Autobiography of Charles A. Hentz, M.D.*, Southern Collection, Wilson Library of the University of North Carolina.
[2] *Idem.*

He took snuff in his nose and blew "generous blasts" through a red bandana. Nicholas was first a Roman Catholic and then a Presbyterian, but though he never manifested any marked interest in religion he had the strange habit of stopping anywhere for a moment of prayer—at the door of a classroom, on the street, in the woods, and other odd places.

But on his impersonal, scientific side he was a leader and an authority. As an arachnologist in particular and an entomologist in general he won respect and a following. Dr. Elisha Mitchell wrote to the University of North Carolina trustees that Hentz was "one of the most accomplished entomologists" in the country and was "a man whose fellow will not be found in the whole Atlantic coast." Until Hentz recorded his studies in the woods and fields of Chapel Hill and elsewhere there had never been an accepted work on American spiders. But in Boston, 1875, was published a substantial book entitled *The Spiders of the United States, a Collection of the Arachnological Writings of Nicholas Marcellus Hentz, M.D. Edited by Edward Burgess with Notes and Descriptions by James H. Emerton.* (Hentz was not an M.D. and his middle name of Marcellus was an Americanization of the French Marcellin.) This for years was the standard book of reference in its field, and his collection of specimens was long housed by the Boston Society of Natural History.

Hentz had other talents. He not only furnished the notes for the 250 species of spiders that he catalogued, but he drew and painted many of the illustrations, some in color, and even etched or engraved the plates, all with unsurpassed delicacy and grace.

Hentz was no doubt chosen for the faculty at Chapel Hill

partly because of his French background. He was born at
Versailles, near Paris, in 1797. His father had been a revolutionary deputy who on being proscribed by Napoleon
III's government changed his name to Arnould and in 1818
emigrated to America, where he found life peaceful and
"douce" (sweet, gentle). Hentz had had some experience
serving in a hospital at Val de Grace, France, and after
coming to America tried to extend this by taking medical
lectures at Harvard. But he avoided medical practice and
occupied himself with teaching French, painting miniatures,
and preparing text-books. He was the author of *A Manual
of French Phrases and French Conversation,* Boston, 1822,
and of *A Classical French Reader,* Boston, 1831. He occasionally tried his hand at verse and is even credited with
writing an obscure novel supposedly patterned after Fen-
imore Cooper's Indian tales. He was for a time instructor at
George Bancroft's Round Hill School at Northampton,
Mass., and was tutor to a family living on Sullivan's Island,
Charleston, S. C.

In 1824 he married at Lancaster, Mass., Caroline Lee
Whiting, daughter of a Revolutionary War officer and member of a large family devoted to each other. He then obtained
the appointment at Chapel Hill and took his young wife and
baby there in 1826. She had never been out of the North
but became a complete Southern partisan, as proved by her
prolific writings. On the journey south by land and sea she
wrote home that he had provided her with a nurse girl to
look after the baby: "I know you will all congratulate me
and feel as grateful to my husband for his solicitude to obtain
me this indulgence." She added that he had shown the
"unremitting care and attention of an appreciative husband."
From Portsmouth, Va., she wrote on the boat to her mother:

"When next you hear from us I trust we shall be safe at Chapel Hill—there were a number of gentlemen and a lady on board, and they all gave a favorable account of that place, the society, climate, etc."

Four years later the honeymoon was still high, for he wrote on June 1, 1830, to his wife from Mason Hall, "ten minutes beyond Hillsborough":

"Where you are not, I am deprived of those dear feelings which alone can make a man happy—I am a cross-grained one, but I am sure you don't know how I love you all."

The term "cross-grained" was the first intimation in his letters that he had become aware of a temperamental instability that worsened through the years until he was at moments little better than a monster, a little monster, for he was only 5½ feet high and weighed less than 100 pounds; but one capable at times of terrifying his family and friends. His son, Dr. Charles Arnould Hentz, believed this defect in his nature was due to the effect on his mother, when pregnant, of the strain of her husband's political persecution in France.

At Chapel Hill the Hentzes found friendship and appreciation, particularly from the Mitchell and Phillips families and from Mrs. Helen Caldwell, wife of the University President. Mrs. Hentz wrote home about the "kindness, warm feeling, hospitality, and union of Chapel Hill." However, Mrs. Joseph Gales wrote from Raleigh to Jared Sparks, the historian, that the Hentzes found the life at Chapel Hill somewhat marred by "the rigid disciples of Calvin." Caroline did not escape sorrow. Her first born, Marcellus, died when less than two years old. Four other children came in due course, Charles and Julia at Chapel Hill, Thaddeus W. and Caroline (Cally) elsewhere.

UNC's First President

"Middle height, eyes dark and penetrating, bushy eyebrows, clothing neat, precise and handsome." This was the way Cornelia Phillips Spencer described President Joseph Caldwell.

Gen. William R. Davie

Commissary General of Greene's Army in the Revolutionary War, Governor of his State and "Father of the University."

South Building—in the Early Days

Called "a palace-like erection, which is much too large for usefulness, and 'Temple of Folly,'" its erection was financed in part by the proceeds from a State lottery.

South Building—in Modern Times

The University Administration, which it has housed for many years, has long since outgrown the "Temple of Folly," and many important offices below the upper echelon have been forced to move into other buildings. Its rear steps (above) also serve as a happy between-classes meeting place for many of UNC's students.

Dr. Elisha Mitchell's grave in the Black Mountain range north-east of Asheville. Standing by is Big Tom Wilson, the guide who found his body in a pool.

Mt. Mitchell Is His Monument

Dr. Elisha Mitchell, who brought the sciences to Chapel Hill, lost his life while exploring the highest peak east of the Mississippi, which was later named for him.

One of the
"razor sharp Winstons"

George T. Winston as
President of the University
met many problems.

Expelled from the
University

Thomas Hart Benton
went west and became a
U. S. Senator and a power in
the administrations of Andrew Jackson and Martin
Van Buren.

Built in Washington's Time

Old East Building—General Davie and the contractor fought over it.

Professor and Expert on Spiders

"One of the most nervous, jealous, suspicious characters that ever lived," was the way his son described Prof. Nicholas Hentz.

Wife and Novelist

"One of the most lovely, sunny dispositions that ever lived," the same son wrote of Caroline Hentz.

Gimghoul Castle

Center of fanciful legends involving duels and tombs.

Prof. B. S. Hedrick

The only professor ever ousted from the University of North Carolina because of his opinions.

Owner of Mason Farm

"An instance of how the broken heart can live on and find something to live for."

II

After six years at Chapel Hill Caroline may have believed their home there was permanent, but if so she received a shock when in 1830 Nicholas announced they would move at once to Covington, Ky., where he would teach at a school for girls. This was the first of five similar uprootings and removals, all in Southern states. In fact, the Hentzes never returned North except for one visit by Caroline to her old home in Lancaster, Mass., after 27 years of absence. If Caroline was ever upset by these repeated removals and her husband's morose habits, she gave no outward sign. She remained amiable and serene as a wife and mother, as a housekeeper for the girls her husband taught, as a teacher in his faculties, and finally as a writer with a national following.

Just when she became a novelist is not clear, but she had apparently tested herself in verse as early as 1820, for her diary recorded that in that year she had received the Philadelphia paper containing her poem, "Rubens the Unknown Artist." In 1833 appeared *Lovell's Folly*, which had a special interest for Chapel Hill on account of its characters. One of these was George M. Horton, the black slave poet, who wrote amative verses for University students for a small fee. Of him she wrote:

"I have often transcribed stanzas which he would dictate with quite an air of inspiration; and have marvelled at the readiness with which he would change a verse or sentiment which was objected to as erroneous in expression or deficient in poetical harmony, and though familiar with best classic works belonging to the fine libraries of the University, he had not been taught to write a legible hand and was obliged to be indebted to others for embodying the dreams of his muse."

She quoted in *Lovell's Folly* this poem by Horton:

> Oh Liberty! Thou golden prize,
>   So often sought by blood,
> We crave thy sacred sun to rise,
>   The gift of Nature's God.
>
> Bid Slavery hide her meagre face
>   And barbarism fly—
> I scorn to see the sad disgrace
>   In which enslaved I lie.
>
> Dear Liberty! upon thy breast
>   I languish to respire,
> And like the swan unto her nest
>   I'd to thy smiles retire.
>
> Deep on thy pillar, thou mortal dame,
>   Trace the inscription of eternal fame;
> For bards unborn must yet thy works adore,
>   And bid thee live when others are no more.

Also in *Lovell's Folly* was a character named "November," a clear recollection of "Dr." November, black coachman for Dr. Caldwell, President of the University. (See chapter entitled "Honor to Black Servants.")

Second in interest to Chapel Hill was Caroline's 1856 novel, *Marcus Morland, or The Planter's Northern Bride.* Much of it was clearly due to her personal experiences. It was also taken as a reply and offset to Harriet Beecher Stowe's *Uncle Tom's Cabin*, published in 1851. A review in the New York *Mirror* said of Caroline's book: "It cannot be read without a moistening of the eyes, a softening of the heart, and a mitigation of sectional and most unchristian prejudice." Aided by this novel, any reader could see that in the widening chasm between North and South, Caroline's sympathies lay on the Southern side. And this enhanced her popularity in the University village. In the novel the chief villain was an abolitionist missionary while the hero, Morland, was a Southern planter, self-contained and stern, but humane in his instincts and just in his actions. In one passage he is painted as turning his thoughts "to the enslaved children of Africa, and taking them as a class, as a distinct race of beings, he came to the irresistible conclusion that they were the happiest subservient race that were found on the face of the globe." This was the view of most slave-holding families—that slaves were not only well treated but were happy.

But the Massachusetts-born author went even further. In her preface she wrote: "During our residence in the South we have never witnessed one scene of cruelty or oppression, never beheld a chain or a manacle, or the infliction of a punishment more severe than parental authority would be justified in applying to filial disobedience or transgression."

The figure of Morland, the hero, was highly idealized, and Caroline's language and style were in accord with this pastel portrait and with the sentimental tastes of the times. The dialogue between her chief characters was stiff and elevated while her handling of the whole Southern scene was colored by the author's own romantic feelings. If, however, her male characters were often stilted, her women were lifelike and feminine, her children convincing.

More realistic were her descriptions of life among Southern rural whites. For example, a country cabin consisted of one room with a bed in each corner. Two of the beds had white counterpanes but the other two were covered only with patchwork quilts. The "crowning glory of the table" was a dish of bacon and greens flanked by "tremendous hoecakes," a cold sweet potato pie, and gingerbread cakes "as large as cheeses." The center candlestick was fixed in a gourd of beeswax and tallow. It was in her rendering of Southern rural and Negro dialects that Caroline fell short, showing that she had not been to the manner born. But these defects did not trouble the stratum of readers whom she acquired. They showed they cared only for romance and not at all for accurate realism.

Her novels grew in popularity as fast as they were published. She had periods when she wrote, wrote, wrote with the concentration of a devotee, sometimes completing two scripts a year and loading her publishers in Philadelphia with manuscripts, all daintily hand-written. Her industry as a writer was possibly due to two factors. One was the need for more family revenue in addition to the moderate earnings of her husband as a scientist and teacher. The other was the need for an orderly and sunny world not marred by the vulgarities of daily life or the demands of an unpredictable husband. Her friends used to say she was capable of withdrawing from a gossiping group in order to write a sudden chapter.

The list of her books includes not only the two novels mentioned but *Aunt Patty's Scrap Bag, Mob Cap, Linda, Rena or Snow Bird, Wild Jack, Helen and Arthur,* and her last work, *Ernest Linwood.* She also contributed to periodicals such as *Godey's Lady's Book,* the *Western Monthly,* and the *Hillsborough Recorder.* In addition, she wrote plays and verse. In many of her fictional works the theme of jealousy furnished a strong but veiled undercurrent.

III

From Covington, the restless Hentz moved his family across the river to a school for girls in Cincinnati. Here Caroline was delighted by an invitation to join a literary group called the Semi Colon Club headed by Dr. Daniel Drake. It put on her play called "Lamoran" which ran for three nights. At one time this group had as a member Harriet Beecher, then 22 years old. She was not yet Mrs. Stowe, author of *Uncle Tom's Cabin*. Did this novel set Caroline's imagination afire in opposition?

Another member, a Colonel King, one day in 1834 wrote Caroline a note, contents undisclosed. Nicholas heard about it but saying nothing, pretended he was going hunting. He returned suddenly and found Caroline writing an answer to the note. He found Colonel King, made a scene, and struck King in the face. Caroline was frightened and ran to Dr. Drake for protection. King carried the incident no further.

Whether this incident or some other incited Hentz's desire for another removal is not known, but he suddenly ordered his wife to pack everything for a move down the rivers to Florence, Ala. On the journey, their son Charles wrote in his autobiography that his mother wept while his father talked grimly of separation. At Florence Hentz bought a shaky school for girls, added a library building, and built a laboratory for himself in which he raised silkworms. It was the time of a popular and daffy belief about the fortunes to be made raising silkworms and selling their fiber. Though Caroline was skeptical, Hentz's experience in entomology was a decided help in the business, and before the craze ended he sold his worm collection for a nice sum.

It was one of the oddities of Hentz's character that despite his difficult temperament, he had a shrewd business sense and was capable of making profitable deals. His silk-worm sale and the disposal of his spider collection, including 250 species, to the Boston Society of Natural History for a pleasant amount, gave him the funds with which he and Caroline built up the Locust Dell Female Academy at Florence to the point where they had 25 to 30 boarding students and 100 day students. The burden of feeding and caring for all these girls fell chiefly on Caroline. A description of the school says there was not a cook stove on the place. The cooking must have been done in old fashioned fireplaces, probably relying on pots and skillets wielded by black servants.

Hentz found the insect life in Alabama plentiful and exhilarating. Daily he took his sons bug hunting, armed with hatchets and vials of alcohol. He even drafted Caroline as a helper as proved by the entry in her 1836 diary: "I shall always look upon the North American Insects, copied from Oliver, as the most interesting of all, because it has been a labor of love." But another entry dated Feb. 7, 1836, sounded a sadder note. On hearing the first bluebird warble of the year she wrote: "I remember a year ago, on a Sunday morning like this, hearing the first notes . . . but it had then no music to my ears. The chords of my heart rang to discordant sounds. Let me be grateful to my Maker that it is now turned to greater harmony." She confesses to being occasionally "borne down by despondency" and added this note as if to lift her own spirits:

"I do love to write home, conscious of the happiness I

am imparting to the warm, affectionate, confiding hearts who bear me in such fond remembrance."

IV

These entries were the first recorded evidence that her life of strain and uncertainty was beginning to wear down her resilient nature. But the end was not yet. As her son Charles wrote: "Father was a rolling stone," and in 1843 he suddenly gave orders that the relatively smooth existence in Florence, lasting eight years, was to be abandoned and everything was to be moved to Tuscaloosa, Ala., where he was to head the Alabama Female Institute.

The trip was made in a carriage with a carryall behind. But Hentz's restless disposition was not stayed and in less than two years he went to Tuskegee, Ala., and took over a girls' school from an owner who wanted to sell. The prospect made Caroline uneasy; she had heard that the Tuskegee pupils were coarse and hard to control. But the truth proved otherwise, and Caroline was happy to write home, "We really have some most charming, intelligent and loveable children." But after a few weeks she wrote her son Charles, who had gone to Louisville, Ky., to study medicine:

"I feel very tired and have just indulged in one of those rare fits of crying which do me so much good."

She had reason to weep, for about this time Hentz, whose paranoia was becoming gradually worse, no longer tried to conceal the fact that he was a regular user of drugs. By 1849 he was a steady consumer of morphine. As a supposed M.D. he could procure any quantity of the drug, which he put up in small packets and kept before him as he worked in his laboratory, taking so many doses a day.

Part of the journey to Tuskegee was made by steamer from Mobile. On this voyage Caroline had made notes which she now used to write a novel she called *Linda, or the Young Pilot of the Belle Creole,* published in 1850.

Tuskegee proved to be only a temporary stop and Hentz's restless fever drove him next to Columbus, Ga., where Caroline first became acquainted with "Georgia crackers," naive and ill-schooled rural inhabitants who at times suffered from chills and fever. She quotes them as saying of malaria, "We don't call that sickness. Shake a little one day, up and smart as a pipestem the next."

Her son Charles, who was moving as a medical graduate from Louisville to Marianna, Fla., came to visit her. He found her "unchanged—as lovely as ever." His father, on the contrary, he found more nervous and irritable than before. On going to the bedroom where his father lay "haggard and wasted," he was appalled. In Dr. Hentz's own words, "I threw myself on his bed, threw my arms around him and sobbed as I never did in my life before." He then realized that his father's career and health were at an end. His mother told him her own career as a teacher was over and that she was confining herself to writing. "I sometimes fall into hypochondriac fits," she wrote Charles. "I feel as if there were no one in the whole world to love me."

The school at Columbus had to be given up and the Hentzes in 1853 moved to Quincy, Fla., where their son-in-law, Dr. Keyes, gave Nicholas a home while Caroline in her 48th year went to live with Dr. Charles Hentz in Marianna. She then had her first opportunity to visit her old home in Lancaster, Mass. The house, occupied by a sister, was the same, but her mother was long gone. On her return south she finished her novel, *Ernest Linwood*. The work seemed to exhaust her. Her strength waned but she rallied long enough to write one more story, "No Cross, No Crown." Dr. Hentz was at her bedside when she died quietly in 1856. *Ernest Linwood* came out the day of her death. Her husband lived a few months longer. They were buried in the Episcopal church yard in Marianna.

"Military Academy" at Chapel Hill

On the south side of Gerrard Hall, which was for years the University chapel, a rainy day or spell of moisture brings out beneath the paint in letters two feet high the words:

WINSTON'S MILITARY ACADEMY

These words have evidently been repeatedly painted over, but because they were originally of a brilliant and lasting red, a wet day makes them stand out. They were lettered there during the "gay nineties" by resentful students. The man these words were aimed at was George Tayloe Winston, who became President of the University in 1891.

George T. Winston was a lover of the classics, especially the Latin classics, and he venerated ancient Rome because it stood for two things he most admired: authority and discipline. He was well liked as a professor, but as a University president he found he could not do as Romans did—run things by giving out orders from above. His tendency to do so led to resentment, and then the students revolted and painted his name ironically on campus buildings. They especially resented interference with their most treasured activity—games and sports, especially football. And they objected to the policing of dormitory life.

There had been bad blood between University athletic fans and the athletes and fans of other institutions in the State, and the University trustees tried to cure the situation by throwing out the baby with the bath, that is, they forbade all forms of intercollegiate athletics. Their action incensed the students. They accused President Winston of inciting the trustees. Hence the lettering in red—the color of blood.

The students sent a committee of three to see President Winston and demand a repeal of the obnoxious ruling. The administration agreed that students might well participate in such decisions and set up an advisory committee of three to pass on all such matters in the future—one faculty member, one graduate student, and one undergraduate. That healed the immediate difficulty, but it did not entirely cure Dr. Winston of his chief failing, a tendency to act like a Roman emperor, to hand down decrees rather than requests.

That he was an able man no one could deny. He proved it throughout his presidency. He greatly increased the student population at the University. He reduced, but did not entirely abolish, the denominational enmity of the Protestant churches against the University. He brought to Chapel Hill able men who strengthened the faculty. He revived the dormant summer school idea which allowed women as well as men to get a taste of higher education. He was prophet of the necessity of more industry to balance the State's agricultural life. He made a lethargic and distrustful people conscious of the value of the University as head of the State's educational structure and showed them why it should expand its activities.

George T. Winston was born at Windsor, Bertie County, in 1856. His natal day was October 12, which could have been taken as a prophetic hint, for at Chapel Hill this is always celebrated as University Day. He belonged to a brilliant family—Cornelia Phillips Spencer, Chapel Hill historian, called them "those razor-sharp Winstons." They included his father, Patrick Henry Winston, Patrick, Jr., Francis D. and Robert W. Winston.

Dr. Winston when a student at Chapel Hill in 1868 was unable to complete his four years there because the University was closed by an adverse State government at Raleigh headed by a renegade secessionist. Winston won an appointment to the Annapolis Naval Academy and was head of his class there. Thence he moved to Cornell, where he was graduated in 1874 and where he was for a time an instructor in mathematics. The next year he was elected adjunct professor in the College of Literature at Chapel Hill, teaching Latin and German at $1,500 a year. Here he was an active member of the faculty under President Battle. When the latter resigned in 1891, Dr. Winston succeeded him, becoming one of the youngest university presidents in the nation.

At his inauguration his friend Walter H. Page, Raleigh editor and subsequently ambassador to Great Britain, addressed these sentiments to the State which were no doubt welcome to Winston's ears: "Renounce forever all servitude to ecclesiasticism and partyism," and make "our long slumbering land a resounding workshop."

Almost at once President Winston put this advice into execution. But he was too astute to make a frontal attack on the dominant and conservative churches of the State. He preferred a flank approach and responded quickly to invitations from semi-religious and semi-political organizations to take part in speech-making occasions. The pulpits of the State watched him closely, for they were gathering their energies for a battle with the University as a rival of their denominational schools. The University, they pointed out, had the benefit of funds donated by the State out of tax money. (The State appropriation for the Winston biennium 1890-92 was $22,500. In ten years it had climbed to this amount from $5,000 annually for four years, 1881-85.)

The battle with denominational leaders had begun in 1881 during the presidency of Dr. Battle, who appealed to the State legislature for an unprecedented annual appropriation of $5,000. He sent Professor Winston down to Raleigh to present the University's case. The sum was granted. The denominational leaders and press greeted the news as equal to a fire alarm. They saw this tiny appropriation as setting a precedent dangerous to their institutions. The University at this time had 166 students; of these 89, owing to an arrangement between the University and county commissioners, paid no tuition. The University was so weak, financially speaking, as to be virtually gasping for breath.

But its critics did not draw their sharpest weapon until Winston had succeeded Battle as president in 1891. Then was born a battle between Church and State such as shook North Carolina in every social stratum and left a welter of resentment. It was still going when President Winston wrote apologetically to Mrs. Spencer: "A tired and nervous man desists from writing friendly and social letters; hence my long and apparently discourteous silence."

The battle had not reached its crescendo when in 1893 a financial and economic panic overwhelmed the United States. North Carolina as one of the most rural of all the states suffered from precipitous falls in the price of cotton and other crops. Out of this crash rose the Populist Party as a form of protest against political control by landowners, merchants and bankers. It wanted to help the farmers; it had small interest in the University. When it joined forces with the Republican Party, then called "radical," it appeared that the University must again do what it had been forced to do in 1868—close its doors. For it could no longer live on what had sufficed it up to now—on the students and their fees.

In April, 1895, President Winston wrote Mrs. Spencer that "it is all over." Not so. The opposition to the University and its aid from the State was bringing up its heaviest guns. But this was as yet not visible to Winston, who wrote to her:

"It is impossible to Tillmanize a state with such a University as ours, vigorous and growing. The University men in the legislature were faithful, else the University were gone today and the state handed over to pigs and pigmies. Even with their aid we came near destruction . . . I have eaten several measures of Mother Earth, and the great strain of nerves and mind and digestive penance has left me badly weakened. Read the last one of Montaigne's essays (Book III), and you will find a description of one of my maladies. Yours very affectionately, Geo. T. Winston."

The word "Tillmanize" here refers to the South Carolina leader of an antiaristocracy movement who became Governor of his State and then a United States Senator— Benjamin Tillman.

Winston's optimism was premature. In a few months the denominational leaders who wanted to minimize the University and maximize their own colleges brought the Rev. John C. Kilgo from South Carolina to present their case. With joy Dr. Kilgo sniffed the battle from afar, and he was joined by the *Biblical Recorder* which declared: "Christian institutions are the only institutions for the sons and daughters of mothers and fathers." But the *Recorder* scored a point when it adverted to the fact that the University had 47 teachers for 413 students, while in the common schools a teacher was expected to deal with 40 to 50 pupils at a salary of $30 to $40 a month for four months of the year.

The reply of the University defenders was that the destruction of the University (with its $5,000 a year grant from the State) would not add a day and a half to the term of the common schools. The denominational colleges had the most active orators on their side, but the University had the forceful support of the majority of the State's leading newspapers. President Winston no doubt was indebted to the sage counsels of Editor Walter H. Page, whom he often consulted. The battle went on with increasing heat for the four years from 1893, the year of the panic, to 1897. Luther L. Gobbel, author of *Church-State Relationships in Education in North Carolina since 1776* (Duke University Press, 1938), records some of the epithets hurled across the chasm separating Church from State institutions at this time: "pugnacious," "irritable," "insolent," "dogmatic," "ravings," "traitors," "educational ring," "University gang."

When the Legislature of 1897 convened, it was recognized that this session would be critical. During the election each side had tried to pledge candidates on the issue of University vs. clerical schools. One bill was introduced to repeal entirely the pathetic little State appropriation to the University. It failed. Instead, the States' aid was raised to $25,000 for the biennium. That cooled off the University's opponents; they had vainly expended much time, effort and money, and they needed a pause for recuperation and decisions as to the next tactic. Their leaders went on muttering well into the turn of the century, but they could no longer rally the old church armies. President E. A. Alderman's conciliatory speech at his inauguration in 1896 took all the remaining fury out of the battle. George Tayloe Winston might retire from the presidency feeling, as he wrote Mrs. Spencer, "tired and nervous," but his efforts at both Raleigh and Chapel Hill had won, and his fame now spread to other states.

Winston could look back on his five turbulent years with some pride. Student enrollment had risen from less than 200 to 500. The internal administration had been tightened and strengthened. Professors had been brought in who were efficient as teachers and departmental heads. The sciences had received more attention than was ever previously known in a conservative old state. The Summer School, begun in 1877 under Battle and starved out by a hostile legislature in 1885, was revived and developed, and parallel summer sessions were begun in law, geology, and biology. The library grew under a paid staff. Winston cemented the position of the University as top and head of the State's educational system, and he gave it something like a national position to replace its former provinciality.

It came as no great surprise when in 1896 the University of Texas invited Winston to become its President. Winston, always an ambitious man, accepted with alacrity. By going to Texas he would be rid of the degrading war (in a letter to a friend he called it "a war of wind and filth") about appropriations with denominational spokesmen; he would preside over a university young in years but growing powerfully in wealth and influence; he would have ample scope to carry out plans that had been hampered at Chapel Hill by the State's monetary niggardliness; and he would benefit financially by a double salary, an important item to a father with children to be educated. At Texas he would receive $5000 annually, a sum at that time paid only to corporation executives.

But at Texas he ran into obstacles and opposition. In a wide country still in some parts keeping a frontier psychology, critics thought he spoke in public too much like an Easterner. His logical approaches and intellectual treatment of far-ranging topics failed to get projects moving. His knowledge of ancient Rome and his devotion to the image of a stern and uncompromising Roman senator seemed out of place in a territory peopled partly by Mexicans, Indians, cowboys, and ranch owners. His forceful and sometimes arbitrary conduct as chairman of official meetings caused barely suppressed mutterings.

But what was worse in its effect on his administration was his disposition to be ruthless in making changes, and his tendency to drop professors without notice and without allowing a defense. These were the very tendencies that had caused the angry reaction of University of North Carolina students when they painted in red letters on the campus chapel the resentful words: "Winston's Military Academy." This label had caused Winston to soften his arbitrary habits during his five years at Chapel Hill, but they cropped out again in the new atmosphere at Texas, and they made new critics and enemies on the Texas board of regents. In three years Winston was finished, and the end of the century saw his end as the University of Texas head.

Fortunately for him an opening was already visible in his native State, and he was not long in returning to North Carolina as President of the A & M College at Raleigh, which later became State College and finally North Carolina State University. Winston's administration at Raleigh was competent, but was handicapped by his lack of experience in either agriculture or mechanics. He made up for this by his zealous approaches to the Legislature, which granted larger appropriations without much argument, and by a firmer internal organization which brought in valuable additions to the faculty and the equipment. Under his hand a technical institute was broadened into a college, but Winston never showed at Raleigh the talents he had revealed at Chapel Hill. The reason no doubt was that his tastes leaned toward the literary and language arts rather than to technology and sciences, and in 1908 he was glad to retire on a Carnegie pension, to travel in Europe, and to rest in the salubrious North Carolina mountains until he had rid his memory of ancient battles and rancors.

But when his health and vigor waned, there was only one place to which his thoughts and recollections most often returned, and that was Chapel Hill. He lived there so quietly in the home of his son Patrick H. Winston, a law professor, that few of the surrounding inhabitants, except surviving contemporaries, knew of his presence. In 1932, when the simple and small University he had known had grown into an ever larger group of stately buildings numbering students by the thousand, he died. He was buried beside his wife on one of the mountain summits at Asheville.

A figure like George T. Winston would probably meet considerable opposition as president of a modern university today. The students who sarcastically painted his name on a campus building in the 1890's were the forerunners of students who in 1968 staged strikes, boycotts, sit-ins and defiance of the police, as testimony to the fact that they were no longer to be treated as children. Able and energetic as he was, George T. Winston would have been a greater university president had he been willing to lead more and drive less.

Honor to Black Servants

I

On the west side of Chapel Hill Cemetery stands a stone shaft eight feet high. It is the only memorial of its kind in the State, in the country, or the world. It was dedicated to the Negro servants of the University by the white students who once enjoyed their services. It bears this inscription:

> Members of the class of 1891 place this stone
> to the memory of
> Wilson Swain Caldwell, who lies here.
> November Caldwell
> David Barham and
> Henry Smith
> Who served the University faithfully.

Of these servants the most famous was "Doctor" November, as he liked to call himself. He considered himself well entitled to be a Doctor since he belonged to the "fambly" of Dr. Joseph Caldwell, first President of the University. Actually he was Dr. Caldwell's coachman, and had charge of "Cuddie," Dr. Caldwell's mule, which regularly grazed in the meadow now grown up into the University Arboretum. Cuddie was at times painted in zebra stripes by students who took him into South Building and tied him there. Dr. Caldwell was a New Jersey man, as explained elsewhere, but when he took up his long residence in Chapel Hill he adopted the Southern custom of buying and owning slaves whom he employed around his house. And "Dr." November was chief among them.

In 1869 when the Ku Klux Klan began to be active around Chapel Hill, the Raleigh *Standard*, organ of W. W. Holden, the turncoat secessionist who had been appointed Governor of the State by the United States government, carried this item about a midnight visit to the University town: "They passed through the street upon horses, making goosey noises. And after enquiring the whereabouts of the negroes and white radicals 'that they were going to shoot K.K.'s if they interfered with them,' and breaking into the houses of Mr. Henry Jones, colored (knowing that he was away from home) and rocking the residence of the notable November, Esq. . . . they retired." It was afterward explained that this attack was due to a mistake.

November did not always bother to live up to the ten commandments, but in 1872 he repented before the pearly gates could close, as recorded in a note written by Mrs. Spencer: "Old Dr. November lies on his death bed. He had made a profession of religion. He told me all about it. He said, 'Miss Cornelia, I liked to have been too late!' His principal pleasure is having some old friend sit and talk about old times. He says he knows he will see all the old faculty sitting up there in heaven. He means to look for 'em!"[1]

Wilson Caldwell, known as "Wilts," whose name heads the list on the monument, was November's son. He was of different nature from his father, being quiet and attentive to duties. A treasured story told about him (and also told about other janitors of the campus) relates to the time when he resigned his University employment to go into the tobacco business in Durham, 12 miles away. In a few weeks he was back at his old employment. When asked about it,

[1] Russell, *The Woman Who Rang the Bell.*

Wilson announced: "Durham ain't no place fer a literary man."

II

Dave Barham was the most dignified man of the lot and as such was often called upon to attend visiting celebrities. He was owned by a white man in Wake County, who rented—the term used was "hired"—him to the University Bursar, Dr. Elisha Mitchell, for an annual fee. Somewhat similarly situated was Sam Morphis, whose owner lived in Texas. Sam "hired his own time" from this owner by an annual payment, an arrangement which was against the law, but in Sam's case it was evaded by an arrangement with John H. Watson, hotel proprietor.

Though these ante-bellum blacks lived under slavery, not a few of them were well-to-do, having profited by tips and by catering to the appetites of students. Dave Moore, for instance, whose place was opposite the old Eagle Hotel on the lot covered subsequently by the Graham Memorial Building, became an owner of much land and cash. When at the end of the Civil War Sherman's bummers came into the village in the wake of 4,000 Federal cavalry led by Brig. Gen. Smith Atkins, Moore hid his money so effectively that after his death no one could find it, and no one ever has.

Another caterer, who was also a part-time barber, was Charlie J. Burnett. He saved his money and bought lots in Oberlin, Ohio, to which he moved his family in order that his children might gain an education.

An extracurricular dish favored by students was a bird supper at 25 cents a head. Such a supper consisted of quail brought in by farmers and hunters, and bought at five cents apiece. When birds were scarce, a meal of pork and eggs would do. Eggs then sold at 10 to 13 cents a dozen. A favorite amusement was to introduce a newcomer to a meal purporting to consist of 'possum or chicken, and then see to it that he was served with stewed owl or boiled cat. This was considered a rare and ingenious form of humor.

The relative prosperity of black household slaves at this period (about 1845) was in contrast to the pathetic poverty of many white families of the county, both before and after the Civil War. For instance, Cornelia Spencer wrote in her notebook concerning a white family of three daughters and two sons living about two miles from Chapel Hill: "They wear the scantiest of homespun or ragged calico, go barefoot, and live on cornbread."

Not belonging to the more prosperous class of Negroes was Benny Booth, who made extra cash by allowing students to crack boards over his head. At first his charge was five cents a crack; but in accordance with the cost of living, this rate was later raised to 15 cents. Benny's head above his ears was high and domed, and the pleasant theory entertained was that it was so solid and thick, no ordinary board could hurt him. Benny was no beggar. He regularly worked as a day laborer and paid his own way. During the late 1890's and the early 1900's he was a prominent figure on Chapel Hill streets and the campus. He allowed himself to be used in the hazing of freshmen by crowing at them like a rooster and flapping his hands at the side of his domed head.

At the turn of the century the most prominent barber in the village, and for a long time the only one, was Tom Dunstan, whose tonsorial shop was next door to Mr. "Hoot" Patterson's store just above the Presbyterian Church. By hearing a student's name he could come pretty close to identifying his home town or county. He loved students and professors and took intense pride in the fact that he belonged to an academic community. His most admired member of the faculty was Prof. M. C. S. Noble, with whom he used to have long philosophic sessions and take buggy rides into the country, sitting side by side behind a veteran nag.

In the 1930's one of the older members of the Negro community was Uncle Jim Holloway, who lived on the ridge above the Durham highway east of the village. He followed the trade of drayman until age and an injury to a leg handicapped him in making a living. He kept himself in food by using two dogs that were quick and effective in treeing 'possums. Jim's captives he kept in barrels and fattened on corn. One day a problem came upon him. A daughter who had parted from her husband came to live with him, bringing three children. The food problem was thus increased, for there were now five mouths to feed instead of one only. And this was during depression days. Uncle Jim solved it by feeding them all on 'possum. He had to increase his nighttime hunts from one a week to two a week. Luckily it was a good 'possum season, his dogs were young, and the woods were nearby. 'Possum for breakfast, 'possum for lunch, 'possum for dinner—that was the menu program at the Holloway home. "Well, we had cornbread too," said Uncle Jim. No one went hungry, no one suffered from malnutrition. All kept well nourished, if not fat. That was the way Uncle Jim brought the family through the depression.

Not to be overlooked are the village's Negro women, those black mothers and aunts who did much to hold Chapel Hill's white families together during the bluest days of the Civil War and after. One of the foremost in her day was

Aunt Easter Snipes, cook for President Battle at "Senlac." She had the weight and figure of a cotton bale, and a heart to correspond. She was the center of a celebrated Chapel Hill story. One day a grandson brought his bride to Dr. Battle's home, for a visit. "Old Prez," as the students called him, invited her to accompany him on his daily walk. A shower came up and wet them slightly. On their return Aunt Easter met them at the front door. She noted their damp footwear. Said she:

"Lawd, Miss Margaret, set right down and let me git them wet stockin's off." The bride complied. Aunt Easter leaned back and beamed.

"Lawd, Miss Margitt, ef I had legs lak dem I'd marry me a man wuth a thousand dollars!"

III

The Chapel Hill black man with the furthest national fame was the poet George M. Horton, who, though a slave and field hand, taught himself first to read and then to write. In this he used castoff books and even printed scraps of paper. His self-training enabled him to write lyric verse for University students who wished to impress their lady friends and eventually to achieve publication in volumes which are now a rarity.

Although identified with Chatham County just below Chapel Hill, Horton was born in Northampton County about 1797. About 1805 his owner, James Horton, moved to a Chatham County farm on which Horton labored as an ignorant "hand." He had a brother who was better favored, probably as a house servant, and who received a little elementary schooling, but George got none. This was in the tradition of the system which forbade all forms of education to slaves. In 1833 James Horton died and his son, Hal Horton, allowed George to "buy his time"—that is, hire himself out and eventually buy his freedom if he could. George now began his own education amid many difficulties, for his mother was a penniless slave with five children, not all of whom had the same father. He used pick-up parts of old spelling books and on Sunday mornings pored over the New Testament and Wesley's hymns. He subsequently wrote about this period thus:

"By close application to my book at night, my visage became considerably emaciated by extreme perspiration, having no lucubratory apparatus, no candle, no lamp, not even lightwood, being chiefly raised in oaky woods." He resisted all temptations to "sacrifice the day in athletic folly, or alibatic levity."

He made a step upward when on Sunday mornings he began to go to Chapel Hill, eight miles distant. There he met University students who gave him old grammars and dictionaries, and even old clothes. Discovering his devotion to rhetoric, they at first encouraged him to recite verses, but later oratory gave place to acrostic verses dedicated to lady friends. He charged 25 cents for a moderate poem, 50 cents for "something warmer." Following is a sample of the love lines that Horton wrote for University students:

> While tracing thy visage I sink in emotion,
> For no other damsel so wondrous I see;
> Thy looks are so pleasing, thy charms so amazing,
> I think of no other, my true love, but thee.

It was a day of distinction when he met President Caldwell. It was perhaps Dr. Caldwell who encouraged him to send a poem to Horace Greeley, editor of the New York

Tribune. Greeley printed it and this increased Horton's prestige.

Another Chapel Hill resident who befriended him was Caroline Hentz, wife of a professor. She was a novelist who, among other books, wrote *Lovell's Folly,* in which a figure representing Horton appears. In a sketch of his life Horton described a very touching scene. Mrs. Hentz had lost a child by death (see chapter on the Hentzes) and Horton went to her with a poem of sympathy. But having not yet learned to write, he could only recite it to her from memory while she took it down. "While thus engaged," he wrote, "she strove in vain to avert the inevitable tear slow trickling down her ringlet-shaded cheek." This vivid passage alone would prove that Horton had gifts as a writer.

In 1829 appeared Horton's first book of poems, *The Hope of Liberty,* published by W. R. Gales of Raleigh. It was the first book by a slave ever brought out in North Carolina and probably in the South. Even in the North there was only one Negro poet of quality—Phillis Wheatley. A second book by Horton appeared in 1838. Prof. Collier Cobb, who made a study of Horton's works, thinks that in this period he published poems in the *University Magazine,* but they were signed by student names.

In April, 1865, when at the end of the Civil War Federal forces occupied Chapel Hill, Horton made another white friend when he met Capt. W. H. S. Banks of the 9th Michigan Cavalry Volunteers, and Banks helped him to the publication of his book, *Naked Genius,* printed by W. B. Smith & Co. at Raleigh. The only surviving copy of this is in the Boston Athenaeum. In North Carolina the final edition of his poems appeared when Dennis Heartt, the Hillsborough printer and editor, published *The Poetical*

Works of George W. Horton, the Colored Bard of North Carolina, to which is prefixed the Life of the Author written by himself.

Horton's last years were woeful to his friends. He went north with Captain Banks and from 1866 to 1883 seems to have lived in Philadelphia. He took to drink and died there in 1886.

Horton's poems were heavily charged with sentiment and the flowery language popular at the period. He was no doubt strongly influenced by the white poets who depended on rhetoric and rhyme to reach readers. He sometimes dipped into the grotesque, as in the title: *Troubled with the Itch, and Rubbing With Sulphur.* But he at times achieved a fine lyric beauty in particular lines and passages, and his achievement was very great when one recalls that he began as a slave and field hand and never learned perfectly either to read or write.

Not Reached by Rail

Chapel Hill has for years been one of the important towns in North Carolina that can not be reached by passenger train. Freight comes in by rail, but not passengers. The absence of passenger train service puts Chapel Hill back into its position prior to 1882 when a railroad spur was built to the outskirts of the village from the main line of the Southern Railway between Durham and Greensboro. The sound of the first locomotive whistle at the edge of the community was greeted with acclamations, for it promised to end the long isolation imposed by the University trustees in the fond belief that thereby the students would be walled off from devilment. They failed to foresee that the students would furnish their own.

The other end of the railroad spur was marked by a station called "University," a place of desolation that deceived passengers relying on ticket agencies and travel promoters. "University" had no population and no traffic except an occasional farm wagon. But since it seemed logical to book Chapel Hill-bound people to "University," innocent passengers were made to suffer, like the Boston editor's wife who brought her son down to enter the freshman class. She was let off the mainline train under a burning sun and remained there four bewildering hours until the little Chapel Hill train under Captain Smith came tooting up and rescued her.

These and other incidents of life in Chapel Hill during the 1880's are recorded by James Lee Love in his short history called 'Tis Sixty Years Since. Mr. Love was well qualified to speak of the period, since he was president of the Class of 1884, became an assistant professor of mathematics, going later to Harvard to teach the same subject. He married June, the only child of Cornelia Phillips Spencer. He was a benefactor of the University in many ways, both during his active years and during his retirement.

He was a witness and participant of the exertions made under Presidents Battle and Winston to rescue the University from the stasis that beset it during the long period of poverty that followed the Civil War. He remarks, "There was no flowing water in Chapel Hill houses," and few bathtubs. Students craving a shower bath in warm weather rigged up a system of V-troughs leading from a spring on Cobb's Terrace and stood under it in Adam's costume, filling the air with shrieks as the chilled water struck naked shoulder blades.

Despite primitive conditions the University heads did not forget their obligations to the rising sciences, and Professor Love describes the first attempt at an observatory. Across the Raleigh road from what is now the Cornelia P. Spencer dorm for coeds was a large lot containing at least two acres. At its center was a plain two-story house, with the kitchen separated from it, where President Joseph Caldwell lived during the latter part of his administration and where President David L. Swain lived throughout his term, 1835-68. The little brick office used by these presidents stood near the gate on the west side of the lot. It was saved from fire in 1886, and was used thereafter as a home for students.

What Mr. Love called "an essential house in Chapel Hill" was John H. Watson's Hotel, later Pickard's Hotel, resting on what later became the site of the Graham Memorial Building. This hotel had two features that made it both a village and a University center. In front it had a wide and roomy front porch fitted with rocking chairs from which loafers and other observers could watch the passing throng of half a dozen unhurried people and which was the terminus and waiting point for hacks coming from Durham or from the railway station in what later became Carrboro.

The other feature, much prized, was the back portion of the hotel which had been extended into rooming quarters with a double porch stretching along the walk to Old East Building. Here bachelor instructors and professional students could obtain room and bountiful board for $15 a month. At the turn of the century board alone at Pickard's cost $12.50 a month, which seemed luxurious as compared with Commons Hall which furnished board at $8 a month.

On the campus of the University in the 1880's there was sparse comfort and not much convenience. Students were accustomed to a Spartan regime and since they spent as much time as possible out-of-doors, they were satisfied with elementary furniture in their dormitories and rooming houses. Central heating and plumbing were not known on the campus until the Carr Dormitory was built at the beginning of the century. Students who wanted to keep warm bought their own wood and built their own fires in brick fireplaces. Water, a bucket at a time, was brought to their rooms by black janitors. It was not uncommon in winter for students to break the ice in their pitchers and pails in order to wash their faces before hurrying to breakfast or to their first class.

Morning prayers were compulsory at Gerrard Hall, and there was a race each day to reach it before the doors closed. The students living in Old East held the record for

speed. It was said that they could jump out of bed at
8:22 a.m. when the warning bell sounded, wash faces, dress,
shave, lace their shoes, gather their textbooks, and cross the
campus in time to catch the first hymn in Gerrard Hall at
8:30. Some of them wore pajamas or nightshirts under the
long overcoats then in fashion.

In most dormitory rooms easy chairs and stuffed furniture were unknown. Instead, rocking chairs with a
cushion in the bottom were favored, and study was carried
out and papers written on lapboards stretched across the
rocker arms. The University Library, which was consol-
idated under the supervision of Mr. Love in 1886, was not
then large enough to accommodate all the students who
might want to study in it. Mr. Love, who was a studious
man, remarks in his short history, "In all my years of college
I never went to the University Library for a book; and I am
sure that was the story of most other students."

The Library was then housed in Smith Hall, which later
became the Playmakers' Building. On the field stretching
out from its southeast corner the students practiced their
athletic sports, of which "choose up" football was prominent, allowing as many as 40 men on a side. There was no
ground for either baseball or tennis, and it was not until
1884 that the first attempt was made to form a track team.
In 1888 came the first intercollegiate football game. It was
played with Trinity College, ancestor of Duke University,
and employed a round ball.

The two student literary and debating societies, the
Dialectic and Philanthropic, received far more attention then
than they did subsequently. In fact, they formed one of the
centers of student life on the campus. They occupied roomy
and well-furnished halls, they had on their walls portraits

of prominent men painted by distinguished artists, and they set up and preserved their own discipline. These societies not only taught a student how to prepare for a debate, but they showed him how to use his body and voice, how to face a critical audience, and how to match wits on the floor. They were an invaluable influence in molding young fellows with a frontier psychology into orators and debaters with some skill and poise. They furnished leaders and lawyers for the State for many years. They declined in influence when oratory and debate themselves declined, and when the automobile came along to disperse the population.

Professor Love reminds us that in the early 1880's there were at the University of North Carolina eight professors and eight college buildings. Writing in 1945, he said: "The Franklin Street front of the Campus of the University of North Carolina at Chapel Hill looks today much as it did 60 years ago. The Caldwell monument was there, but the Civil War soldier has been added. The Davie Poplar showed a damaged top, from a lightning stroke in 1873, and it leaned considerably toward the East. Many trees have been added, and the whole region from South Building to the Street has today the look of being well cared for, which it lacked then. There was no money for its upkeep; and all that we could do for this beautiful area was to mow the tall grass and wild flowers with a scythe.

"The two North-South walks from the Old East and Old West buildings were as inviting then as now; and the 'President's Walk,' crossing from the old Raleigh road to the Old West walk, seemed to us incomparably romantic. The plot on which stands the Davie Poplar and the Caldwell monument was 'forbidden ground.' The Dialectic and Philanthropic Societies each imposed a fine upon any member

if he entered and crossed this part of the Campus. Each
Society imposed a fine also upon anyone who sat upon, or
walked over, the terraces around the bases of the Old East
and Old West buildings. These fines seemed primarily for
the purpose of adding to the book funds, and served us
well; for until 1886 the Society Libraries were the only ones
usable by students."

Professor Love's short history is a reminder that for 10,
even 20 years, after the Civil War, the University crept along
in a state of poverty. In this it was only reflecting the
poverty of the State, which was not for another 20 years ready
to make the transition from dependence on a plantation
system of agriculture to reliance on a growing degree of industry; that is, from furnishing raw materials like cotton to
manufacturing finished goods. It is to be noted that Mr.
Love and his son, James Spencer Love, showed the way by
the creation of Burlington Industries, which is now inter-
national in its properties and operations.

In 1875 when the University was reopened under President Battle after a five-year suspension, Mr. Love remarks
that Battle's "only sure income was $7500 a year from the
so-called Land Grant Act of the United States Congress.
To this he could add the small tuition fees of students and
the smaller fees for room rent." At this time the General
Assembly of the State contributed nothing to the University's support. Chapel Hill fed on itself. But here again
the Legislature was only reflecting the mood of the State,
which, in the words of University President E. A. Alderman, was "subject to hurtful spasms of economy." Many
years passed before the State and its Legislature could recover from the habit of looking back and judging everything
by its past poverty and inertia.

References have been made to the keen value of Mrs. Cornelia Phillips Spencer's writings about older days in Chapel Hill. There have been, besides, other chroniclers from the University faculty whose written recollections are scarcely less indispensable.

First in order of time is Prof. William Hooper, who in 1859 made before an alumni gathering an address which he call *Fifty Years Since*. He was the grandson of William Hooper, signer of the Declaration of Independence, and he was builder of the house at East Franklin and Battle Lane which in modern times became known as the Kyser House. He was a teacher of ancient languages.

He "first knew" Chapel Hill in 1804 when the students of the University numbered sixty; to preside over them were two professors and one tutor. The only finished buildings were the "East Wing" as Old East was then known, and the Old Chapel, later called Person Hall. The two literary societies, Dialectic and Philanthropic, held regular meetings in the Old Chapel without heat and with winter winds sometimes sweeping through broken window panes.

Board could be had at Steward's Hall, a wooden structure seated between what is now the Playmakers' Theatre and the Carr Building, for $35 a year. Dinner at noon consisted of cornbread and bacon, "with coleworts." Breakfast was bread, butter and coffee. Supper was coffee and any leftover cornbread. In homes it was dangerous to leave anything edible exposed, for ravenous students, roaming the village after dark, would fall upon it and consume it to the last morsel. The richer students could go out to "Fur Craig's," situated about where the Carrboro line now is, and get a chicken dinner for 25 cents.

Another valuable chronicler, who brings up the record

to the 1960's, was Albert C. Coates, law professor and
founder of the Institute of Government, who in 1969 issued
a bound volume entitled *What the University of North
Carolina Meant to Me: A Report to the Chancellors and
Presidents and to the People with whom I have loved and
worked from 1914 to 1969.* Coates was a farm boy born in
Johnston County in 1896. In 1914 he came to Chapel Hill as
a self-help student and was employed part-time in the office
of the University business manager, Charles T. Woollen. At
that time the University had 800 students. They numbered
1000 in Coates' junior year. President of the University then
was Edward K. Graham (not to be confused with later
president, Frank P. Graham [died 1972], though the two
men were cousins).

Coates names as the "most significant and valuable student activity" in his day the meeting and debates of the
two literary societies, the Philanthropic and the Dialectic.
He belonged to the former, which had 150 members. He
mentions those members of the faculty who most influenced
him: Foerster, F. P. Graham, Cobb, Baity, Greenlaw, Williams, Bernard, Branson, Raper, Henderson, Wilson, Coker,
and Mangum, not omitting Woollen, the business manager.

After graduation in 1918 Coates considered other employment but decided in favor of the Law School and never
regretted it. His experiences there caused him to see the
need of greater cooperation between state, county and mu-
nicipal governments and departments which caused him to
organize the Institute of Government in 1933. Its first building was dedicated in 1939. It has become nationally famous.

Dealing with the lighter side of student life in his day,
Coates mentions two activities. One was the night singing
in good weather on the sward between the Old East and

Old West buildings, and the daily gathering at the old post office, where the supposed purpose was to collect one's mail, but since few students could expect any, the real purpose was social.

Taken together the written recollections of these chroniclers, cover 165 years. When taken seriatim they form a social history not only of the University of North Carolina but of the village that grew up around it. In the former case there has been a growth in this period from an enrollment of 60 students to more than 18,000, while a village of a few hundred souls has grown into a township having more than 30,000 inhabitants. And each history is full not only of reliable data but of the affection which both University and town have always inspired in those who have known them longest and best.

North Carolina's Po' Boy Painter

Visible at Raleigh in the State Library and the Supreme Court Chamber, and in University buildings in Greensboro and Chapel Hill are portraits painted by a North Carolina po' boy, William G. Randall. He was so poor that he could not afford the fare from his Burke County home to Chapel Hill, so he walked. At the University he was both befriended and ridiculed. He arrived there in 1879 with 30 cents in his pocket, but he stayed, studied, graduated, and went on to make a name for himself, both in his native State and abroad.

Randall got his training as a pedestrian when in his 'teens he walked daily from his home to the nearest free school three and a half miles distant. He worked as a farm hand till he was 19 years old, beginning when he was too small to lift a plough and was forced to drag it around at the end of each furrow. He got improved instruction at the old academy lying in the shadow of Table Rock, but was still unable to meet the entrance requirements when he reached the University.

Randall left a detailed account of his journey from his home on "the Taylor place" near Piedmont Springs in Burke County to Chapel Hill in November, 1879. He had a friend at the University who probably encouraged him to come, foot or train or both. (This student has been identified as Robert Sevier McCall of Asheville, who was a law student at the University in 1879-80. He was at one time solicitor for Buncombe and four other western counties.) Randall teamed up with another youth, a cousin, who was going to Trinity

College in Randolph County, on a small capital. Randall had just three dollars.

"We got some bread and meat for lunches," wrote Randall, "bundled up some clothes, and set out to walk late one afternoon. We walked about 10 miles and slept on some planks in an unfinished schoolhouse by the roadside."

Next day they passed through Lenoir in Caldwell County and made 35 miles. "At dark we were tired, and feeling low in spirits we tried to get shelter at some of the houses on the road and were turned off again and again, till at last about 9 o'clock we were taken in and slept in a bed that night."

Wilkesboro was their next stop. Here they learned that a train from Winston to Greensboro could be caught the next afternoon. By this time Randall's valise had become so heavy that a train ride was enticing and they headed briskly for Winston. But at dark Randall's legs gave out. They made a fire in the woods and lay until midnight in a pile of shavings left by a sawmill. By that hour Randall was feeling strong again and they resumed the march. They crossed the Yadkin River at daylight and reached Winston in time to catch the train. They fell into a coach tired and footsore. At Greensboro they parted, the cousin going on to Trinity where, however, he remained only a few weeks. Randall walked on alone.

"I found a grove not far from the depot," he wrote, "scraped up some leaves and lay down with my valise for a pillow at the foot of a large oak. I did not sleep soundly. I felt the chill and heard the shrieks of the November wind even in my dreams." The next morning he found a brook and washed his face in it. "I was ashamed to be seen washing at any of the town pumps." For breakfast he bought two sandwiches for ten cents "and had a feast." He got a train to Hillsborough and from there walked the 14 miles to Chapel Hill, still lugging his valise. He arrived about 4 p.m.

"I had heard such great tales about students there that I expected to be tarred and feathered as soon as I made my appearance. I walked through the gate and up the walk toward the New East with my heart in my mouth." He questioned a little Negro as to where he might find his friend McCall but the urchin was too frightened to reply. A campus servant led him to McCall, who took him in and lent him some money.

Luckily he met President Kemp P. Battle. "I knew," he wrote later, "the moment I saw his face that I would get sympathy and encouragement." He was not deceived. Through President Battle he got work to do and financial help from the Deems Fund, which had been established by a former faculty member, later pastor of the Church of the Strangers in New York. (See chapter on "Vanderbilt Helps U.N.C. Students.") He got other help.

"The first overcoat I ever owned," he wrote, "was a present given me by a member of the faculty in the winter of 1880. It lasted me until the winter of '84 and was good as new then." Even so it was hard to eat and be clothed until he had learned to "club" with other students and get his living expenses down to a few dollars a month.

Randall was skilled with his pen as well as brush. He left this portrait of himself as he reached the campus and registered as a student: "homespun jeans, hickory shirt, no collar, homemade shoes, and old floppy hat." He shrank as he looked at the well-dressed young men from the towns and cities. They had a sharp and knowing air and made the newly arrived mountain boy feel far out of place.

It was the era when the hazing of new students was an annual ritual, and gangs of sophomores who noticed his ungainly figure "freshed" and taunted him, singing: "You're going to get a blacking bye and bye." They made him dance till he could dance no more, and one upperclassman called to him: "Why don't you wear a collar?" (A collar at this period was a conspicuous piece of apparel, high on the neck and forcing the wearer's chin high up.) But Randall records that this man's fellows "hissed and shamed him." In one of these taunting groups was a student who became a member of the faculty and another who became a college president. Randall's status improved when it was found he was clever with paint and crayon. One student paid him $5 for a sketch of himself with a mustache so painted on as to impress his girl. Since a five-dollar bill was a substantial sum at the time, and particularly so to a working student, it may be imagined that from this moment Randall began to entertain dreams of an artist's life. He got a tutor to help him prepare for his freshman year and did odd jobs to pay his way, including keeping the books of the Dialectic Society. He made friends, stood well in his classes and graduated in 1884.

His first job was as a teacher in the academy at Marion, N. C. He did not succeed as a teacher but did something better. He found a wife who encouraged and understood his latent talent. She was an assistant at the school, Annie J. Goodloe of Warrenton. She persuaded him to go to New York and study art. From there he went to South Carolina College at Columbia and taught more briefly. His wife argued him out of further teaching and he opened a studio in Raleigh. Concerning that studio W. E. Christian wrote in the Raleigh *News and Observer*:

"There is a bit of carpet, a half averted bust of Vance on a high shelf, a Meissonier scrap copied from the Luxembourg, Henner's 'Sleeping Nymph,' and Cardinal Lavigerie, literally rebaptized by Bonnat. Then further away on another shelf are chalk plaques of Vance again, and underneath a lifesize portrait of Governor Worth." Evidently at this stage the mountain boy was moving up to a more refined strata in life, and sketches of him made at this time show him to be well dressed and well fed. Portraits painted by him at this period, include one of the Rev. J. P. Mason, donor of the great Mason farm to the University.

From Raleigh Randall moved to Washington, and then to Paris, where he studied at the Julien Academy. From Paris in 1894 he wrote to the *University Magazine* about a Thanksgiving dinner for American artists, 63 in number. Among the French and foreign painters present were such famous people as Bougereau, Laurens, Constant, Whistler, Sargent, Bridgman, Weeks, Munkacsy, Eustis, Reid, Wannamaker, and Mrs. Frank Leslie. Some of these names were, or became, celebrated in art history, a far cry from the time when Randall was still a rawbuck student at the University of North Carolina and was a member of a swimming party at Strowd's Pond where another student on sighting a scarecrow called out, "There's Randall's hat."

Randall returned to Washington and then came back to Raleigh, where visitors often found his studio closed. It became known that his health was failing and he went to Arizona. The disease was in his lungs and when it was not arrested he returned to his native state, and from there to Washington once more, where he died in 1895. In 1943 a portrait of him was unveiled in the Oak Hill School in Burke County, successor to his old school at Table Rock.

This tribute by Randall remains as one of the most impressive ever paid to the University of North Carolina: "It is not a rich man's college. It is a poor boy's college and the State cannot spend money in any other way that will make such large returns."

"Mr. Sam" and His Stucco House

I

On the corner of Franklin and Hillsborough Streets, Chapel Hill, opposite the President's house, is a compact one-story stucco two-room cottage which is unlike any other building in the town and which for many years has been an object of curiosity to newcomers.

This was the pre-Civil War law office and schoolhouse of Samuel Field Phillips, who was Auditor in Governor Zeb Vance's Confederate Cabinet at Raleigh and who a few years later was Solicitor General in President Grant's federal administration in Washington. He kept the same office under Presidents Hayes, Garfield and Arthur.

He was the son of Dr. James Phillips, professor of mathematics in the University, who lived in the Widow Puckett house next door, the same house subsequently occupied by President F. P. Venable of the University and later by former Chancellor R. B. House. And he was the brother of Dr. Charles Phillips, also mathematics professor, who lived on the other side of his father in what became known as the Presbyterian Manse; and of Cornelia Phillips Spencer, historian and legend preserver, who later lived in the bungalow-type house opposite her father's. This group of houses was one of the centers of Chapel Hill life for many years.

The stucco cottage was not only a law office but a schoolhouse. In it Samuel Phillips taught boys not only the rudiments of law but of Latin, Greek, arithmetic, geography, history and English grammar. Among his pupils when he was a very young man were William H. and Richard, sons of Judge W. H. Battle, founder of the University law school. In a report to their father June 26, 1847, Mr. Phillips wrote formally: "My intercourse with both William and Richard is very pleasant, and I have seen nothing in their characters or conduct that demands reprehension."

Just when this cottage was built is not recorded, but it was evidently existing some years before the Samuel Phillips House (long known as the Kluttz House, now the Coenen House) on the same lot was built next door to James Phillips House, for on November 20, 1856 Sue Fetter, living diagonally across the street, wrote Cornelia Phillips Spencer: "Your brother Sam's house was raised today—how nice it will be—Fanny (wife of Samuel Phillips) is so happy at the prospect—now your father has his two sons on each hand." This custom of sons building homes on either side of their father was an old patriarchal one and was long followed in the South.

Even in boyhood young Samuel showed his intellectual ability. At the age of 13 he entered the University and in 1841 was graduated at 17 years, three months, with honors. He won his Master's degree in 1844, and in the same year, as representative of the Dialectic Society, he was one of the founders of the *University Magazine* and for several years was one of the steady writers for it. This magazine is one of the oldest student periodicals in the country, and is still much consulted for its historical articles.

In 1845 Mr. Phillips studied law under Judge William H. Battle, who for a time shared the two rooms in the stucco cottage. Until 1848 the young lawyer taught school and conducted a Latin class in the University. In that year he married Frances Lucas, granddaughter of Governor Stone. Politics attracted him and in 1854 and 1856 he was elected to the House of Commons at Raleigh. When the Civil War came on, he, like many other people in Chapel Hill, was opposed to secession; nevertheless he became the Auditor in Charge of War Claims in Governor Zeb Vance's Cabinet. All through the war he maintained his hope for the restoration of the Union of States, even when in 1865 he was elected Speaker of the House of Commons. In that year the war-tired people on both sides craved some movement toward peace. When on Feb. 3, 1865, President Lincoln and Secretary Seward of the United States went down to Hampton Roads, Va., and met three Confederate delegates named A. H. Stephens, R. M. T. Hunter and J. A. Campbell in a private conference on board the Union transport *River Queen,* Mr. Phillips was among those who urgently hoped for the war's end. But when the Confederate representatives came away, reporting that "the enemy refused to enter into negotiations with the Confederate States . . . or to give our people any other terms . . . than our unconditional submission to their rule," Mr. Phillips was deeply depressed and wrote to former Governor William A. Graham:

"All that class of citizens who, as a last resort and preferable to that fate which stares us in the face, wished to know upon what terms the South might reunite with the North, have been utterly disappointed." Referring to the secessionists he added: "I look for nothing but a prolongation of our misery and a deeper depth of ruin as the fruit of their longer continuance in the management of Southern interests . . . I have very decided convictions as to the future of this war for North Carolina—either a speedy taking of the reins out of the hands of her present rulers—or being overrun by the enemy."

His gloom was well founded, for in less than eight weeks

after the meeting at Hampton Roads the Confederacy had collapsed, and North Carolina, like other Southern states, was in fear that its former slaves would turn upon it. Mr. Phillips did not share this fear. "I desire to be liberal to the former slaves," he wrote, "in every respect not looking to political conditions." He further showed that in a time of entrenched prejudices he favored the breaking up of ancient crusts when at a called meeting of the State Legislature in January, 1866, the war being eight months ended, he argued for the introduction of Negro testimony in courts "except where the parties are exclusively white." He cited the example of ancient Rome, which gradually admitted conquered peoples to most of the privileges of Roman citizenship.

Mr. Phillips was never a slave owner himself, but his father had owned two slaves who were house servants—Ben and Dilsey Craig. Dilsey, after a long period of freedom, came back to resume her servant status and lived to a great age, well looked after by Cornelia Phillips Spencer and by gifts from Cornelia's brother, Samuel. After her death Dilsey's grave in the Chapel Hill Cemetery was marked by an engraved stone erected to her honor by June Spencer Love, daughter of Cornelia and niece of Samuel. It is still there.

II

After the war it was recognized that the University was facing new influences, and in 1867 Mr. Phillips was named on a committee of five to suggest desirable changes. It was found that the old instructional system was top-heavy with ancient languages. It was recommended that more attention be paid to science and commerce. But the University never had a chance to effect these changes, for Gov. W. W. Holden, who had been appointed to office by the Federal Government, and who had long been a critic of Chapel Hill, closed the University with soldiers in 1868 and weeds grew about its doors for nearly five years.

Actually, the University did not close its doors officially to students until February 1, 1871, when it was ordered to do so by action of the Board of Trustees. One student, on learning of the action remarked: "This old University has busted today and gone to hell!"

It was now impossible for Mr. Phillips to support a growing family—he became the father of five children—with a village practice, and he was not blamed when he moved to Raleigh. He was blamed, however, and that heatedly, for deserting his Whig connections and taking part in the activities of the Republican Party. He could not have drawn more fury upon his head had he joined the party of Satan; for North Carolina, like the South generally, was smarting under the humiliation of occupation and disfranchisement, and it blamed the evils of the reconstruction era on the Republican administration at Washington. To Mr. Phillips, however, the Republican Party was the party of union and progress, and he told his friends he could not stomach the "corruption and extravagance" of the Democratic Party which was replacing the upper-class Whigs. His intimates, however, were shaken, and even his beloved sister Cornelia could only write:

"I have too much faith in the head and heart of my brother to be affected by what the newspapers say of him disparagingly."

This was echoed by Kemp P. Battle, Raleigh lawyer and subsequently President of the University, when he wrote to

Cornelia in 1870 concerning her brother's nomination for Attorney General on the Republican ticket:

"He was nominated by the more honest element of the Republican party, headed by Tod Caldwell (afterwards Governor). It was a bitter pill to Holden (Governor of the State, not elected but appointed in Washington).

"I regret as much as you do Mr. Sam's false position before the country. I have not had such pain in years. But he is so truthful and honorable and noble a man he will soon outlive the false impressions of the present day."

On removing his family to Raleigh, "Mr. Sam," as he was generally called, entered a partnership with R. H. Battle and then with Judge A. S. Merrimon, a Republican stalwart from the mountains, who became Chief Justice of the North Carolina Supreme Court.

Mr. Sam did not feel he had made a false move by joining the Republican Party and never assumed a defensive position, however secretly he suffered when he and his family were boycotted socially. In a speech at Concord, N. C., July 4, 1890, he said:

"The Republican party has done a noble work in North Carolina. . . . I speak of it the more freely because I had no part in it. Having been banned (i.e., disfranchised) under the reconstruction acts, I quietly looked on and gave my exclusive attention to my professional business. My vote for General Grant at the election in November, 1868, is the only vote that I have given for political reasons since 1866."

Two years later Mr. Sam was appointed Solicitor General of the United States by President Grant. It was supposed Grant had two main reasons: one was a reward to Mr. Sam for his support of the Republican Party; the other was an effort at national reconciliation by the appointment of a former Confederate official to a high Federal position. This post Mr. Sam occupied for 12 years. It was agreeable to him economically and temperamentally. In it he could devote himself to purely legal studies without the partisan rancors which he hated by nature. Meantime he kept in touch with North Carolina affairs. In February, 1873, he was one of 55 University alumni who met in the Senate Chamber at Raleigh to consider means to revive the University, which was reopened in 1875 with Dr. Kemp P. Battle as President. Four years later it gave the degree of LL.D. to Mr. Sam.

He was an advocate of the summer Normal School at the University, one of the first signs of recognition by the State that girls as well as boys must be educated. Previously women had been allowed to hear an occasional lecture in Chapel Hill, but they had to sit behind a screen.

Despite the distance and his official duties, Mr. Sam, aided by regular letters from his sister Cornelia, kept in touch with Chapel Hill and watched the burgeoning affairs of the University. When in 1887 President Battle came under a wave of criticism, Mr. Sam wrote to Cornelia:

"I regret to hear that a new spout of hot water may have opened upon Kemp . . . The active, benevolent, and beneficent citizen must take what comfort he can from his activity and good works. He will get little or no return of gratitude or kindness from the people whom he serves. I am spending some leisure in reading Irving's *Washington* and therefore am fresh from the worry with which his fellow citizens pursue him . . . There were armies of dyspectics and cranks and Adullamites and malicious folk, perched like vultures on dead trees . . . and these hovered over Washington from time to time, waving their wings."

At another time he wrote concerning Henry Clay, whom

he much admired: "The difference between Mr. Clay's mind and those of his two competitors (Calhoun and Webster), is precisely that between what in common parlance we call a practical mind and minds more or less impracticable. The world is no place for a man who will live logically. Society is a compromise, and all who live in it must comply with its spirit."

Mr. Sam's other way of maintaining links with Chapel Hill was to come down from Washington as often as possible. At such times he came laden with $10 bills and these he distributed through his sister to the destitute folk of the village and countryside who were the helpless victims of the unstable reconstruction era. Cornelia Spencer in a letter to her daughter June thus recorded one of his visits: "When Uncle S. came in last night, before he took off his hat he handed me a bottle of very fine whiskey, saying Col. Ruffin had given it to him . . . I smiled a private smile as I took it."

Near the end of the century Mr. Sam, his first wife having died, married Sarah Maury of Leesburg, Va. Cornelia Spencer, who soon afterwards was a guest at her brother's home, wrote concerning her: "Such pretty ways she has, graceful, playful." About Mr. Sam's residence on K Street, Washington, she wrote: "There are so many handsome things about the house—paintings, vases, bric-a-brac generally."

Cornelia was now living in Cambridge, Mass., and her brother Sam seemed to take extra pleasure in writing to her about recollections of Chapel Hill and old Orange County characters such as "Doctor" November, President Caldwell's black coachman; Ben Craig, his father's former slave; Dave Barham, the University servant; and C. J. Burnett, the barber; also such former white friends as Thomas Hogan, Ithiel Atwater, the Rev. George W. Purefoy, Jennie Pendergrass, and Squire Charles W. Johnston. As Mr. Sam aged his letters rarely mentioned any official events or even family matters; they dealt almost exclusively with old Chapel Hill. When in 1884 he attended in Washington the funeral of John Pool, former United States Senator from North Carolina, he wrote:

"The grave is under a singularly beautiful specimen of cucumber tree, its fruit blooming with a delicate pink. To me it gave a North Carolina touch of color to the occasion. As the attendant took up some dust to emphasize the solemn transfer by the minister I leaned eagerly forward to see it lie upon the coffin, there it appeared, just *appeared*, not thrown enough to rattle—the *'exigui pulveris jactu'* of which Virgil speaks as so potent in the fighting of bees and that has been so eloquently adapted. I think such dust falls upon the hearts of the survivors as well as on the head of the departed."

After the turn of the century Mr. Sam's letters became more and more broody, and those who watched over him at home became anxious about his loss of strength. In 1902 his wife Sarah died, leaving him more alone than ever. The next year his body had visibly aged, though his mind was still clear. Later in the year he sank slowly and died in bleak November, 1903. His last request was that he be buried "in the woods at Chapel Hill." It was granted. The village cemetery was then at a distance from the campus buildings. His body was placed in the Phillips plot near his father, mother, and brother Charles.

"I leaned on him," wrote his sister Cornelia. She added: "My brothers were better men than I was a woman."

The House Shaped Like a Hexagon

More than half hidden among trees and shrubs, near the first bend in the eastward road from Chapel Hill to Durham, is the oddly shaped dwelling known as the Horace Williams House, long occupied by the University's professor of philosophy.

It was designed in the shape of a bee-cell or hexagon, because its original owner, who was a mathematician and chemist, believed that the wise bees knew how to build the strongest structure in nature. The designer was Prof. B. S. Hedrick, who became celebrated as the only professor ever ousted from the University of North Carolina because of his opinions. He was the center of the most violent controversy of his day.

Professor Hedrick was not at all that dreaded figure known as the "agitator." He was mild of manner, rarely spoke in public, and never aired his views on the street. He was content to remain in his laboratory and liked to pore over equations rather than politics. But one day five years before the Civil War, a student came to him and asked him whom he intended to vote for in the aproaching presidential election of 1856. It is not known whether this student acted on his own initiative or was instigated by those heresy hunters who have ever kept telescopes bearing on the University. Mr. Hedrick apparently suspected nothing. In answer to the student's question he said, "Frémont."

This answer turned out to be the match applied to a fuse leading to a powder barrel. To understand the emotions governing the period it must be said that although the Civil

War was five years off, its shadow was already falling over events in North Carolina, which was not a state of great slave owners but which was under their domination scarcely less than the other Southern states which had more slaves and more aggressive slave owners.

In North Carolina the owning class had as its chief spokesman the inflammatory W. W. Holden, editor of the Raleigh *Standard*. Holden was a country boy who came out of nameless obscurity in Orange County to apprentice himself to a printer, who taught him the rending power of the printed word when emotions are near the surface and feverish. Holden had got a pretty good education out of the printshop, though he never had the advantages enjoyed by the students at the University only a few miles away. Whether he resented this circumstance or had other motives is not certainly known, but he early revealed a decided bias against the obvious influence of the University in the direction of conservatism and made his newspaper a sort of weathervane indicating the winds for and against slavery. In the slave-owning states there could be no freedom of opinion or expression, and no discussion of slavery even of a social or friendly nature. This fact gave Holden a tremendous lever for operation. When his sympathizers in Chapel Hill informed him of Professor Hedrick's political intentions, Holden set the match to the powder.

Why did he fasten upon the word "Frémont"? Frémont was an army officer and respectable character; was even a sort of hero as an explorer and discoverer in the far West. But Frémont was the presidential candidate of the Free Soil Party, which wanted all newly admitted states kept free of slavery. In the South the Free Soilers became known as "black Republicans," a term giving rise to violent emotions. These emotions Holden knew how to play upon. In 1856 he wrote and printed in the Raleigh *Standard* an editorial saying:

"If there be Frémont men among us, let them be silenced or required to leave. The expression of black Republicanism in our midst is incompatible with our honor and safety as a people. Let our schools and seminaries of learning be scrutinized, and if black Republicans be found in them, let them be driven out."

It was noted that in the editorial neither Hedrick nor slavery was mentioned, but every one in Chapel Hill knew whom and what was meant. That the *Standard's* statement conflicted with every basic American principle scarcely carried weight with those persons whose emotions had already been stirred up by anti-slavery agitations.

These emotions were further heated by a letter signed "Alumnus" appearing in the *Standard* a few days later. It spoke of a "poisonous influence" at Chapel Hill and of "a canker worm preying at the very vitals of Southern institutions." Hedrick's friends predicted that the next step would be the creation of a mob or mob spirit. This came when Hedrick went to Salisbury to attend an educational convention held in the Presbyterian Church. A raucous gang followed him from the church to his room shouting insults and flourishing a mocking effigy.

Hedrick made the mistake of sending to the *Standard* a long letter stating his position logically; that is, he thought calm logic would offset violent emotions. He said he favored Frémont as a candidate because Frémont had been an "enlarger of science" and a conqueror of California. He declared it had not been his "object to attack the institution of slavery"; his opposition was to the *extension* of slavery into those areas where it had not previously existed. In taking this position, he said, he had been influenced by the example of Washington, Jefferson and Clay.

His use of these sacred names brought on a new outburst of denunciation and name-calling. The University wilted. It appointed a committee of Hedrick's fellow professors which, after praising his ability and character, declared his opinions and actions had been contrary to the "usages" of the University. The trustees followed this with a hint that it would be better for Hedrick to depart forthwith. He did depart and went to Washington to find employment.

In 1861 he was employed in the United States Patent Office. His amazement can only be surmised when in a few years Holden, the fiery advocate of secession and persecutor of Hedrick and all unionists, went over to the "Yankee side" and, as a reward, was named provisional Governor of North Carolina. He employed the military to enforce his closing of the University doors and was finally impeached and deposed.

Hedrick's late critics in North Carolina must have been equally amazed when Hedrick became the virtual determiner in Washington of the political fate of the lately disfranchised citizens of his home state. The administration had no means of knowing what ex-Confederates were worthy of pardon and restoration of rights. Hence about applications from North Carolina Hedrick was more and more consulted. In fact, he was often a caller at the White House where his information was useful to President Johnson's secretaries and assistants. He was regularly in correspondence with Governor Jonathan Worth of North Carolina and his prestige at the White House is proven by his letter to the Governor June 7, 1866 in which he said:

"Whenever there are cases in which it is important that the pardons be issued soon, by writing a note to that effect and sending it to me, I can bring the matter at once to the notice of the President or his Secretary and get speedy action."

The action that frequently followed Hedrick's representation at the White House left no doubt that he had become a power in Washington, a fact that was bewildering to those who had approved his dismissal from the University.

After the war Hedrick acquired not only power but prestige, and was often visited in Washington by these North Carolinians who admired his character though not in accord with his political opinions. Among these visitors was Cornelia Phillips Spencer, whose brother Samuel had likewise become anathema in Chapel Hill because of his changed political affiliations and objection to secession.

At Chapel Hill Hedrick had been considered one of the best-trained men in the University faculty. He had studied mathematics at Harvard and had been befriended by ex-Gov. W. A. Graham, former Secretary of the United States Navy. It was probably Hedrick's mathematical leaning that caused him to design in 1852 his Chapel Hill house in the form of a hexagon (it has been altered since). It was shaped so as to let in the winter sun but ration the summer one.

After being an honor graduate in the University Class of 1851, he had risen to be head of the State Department of Agricultural Chemistry with a laboratory in the basement of the Smith Building, later the Playmakers'. This laboratory was intended to be the nucleus of a school of agriculture and technics which was to become an integral part of the University in Chapel Hill. But the State Legislature moved this nucleus to Raleigh, which in time became North Carolina State College and then North Carolina State University.

After Hedrick's ouster, his hexagon house was occupied by Prof. Hildred Hosea Smith, known as "Tige" by the students who once set a can of powder under his chair and exploded it. Prof. George T. Winston was a still later occupant; he installed an underground dining room in the basement for the sake of coolness in summer.

The occupant who made the house most famous was Prof. H. Horace Williams, teacher of psychology and philosophy, who more than once alarmed the State by unorthodox opinions about wars and governments. He often held classes in his study and was one of the few professors whom students consulted about private problems. Such consultations nearly always took place in this house.

Vanderbilt Helps UNC Students

How did the great fortune of Commodore Vanderbilt, estimated at $100,000,000, come to help the poorer students at the University of North Carolina? How did any part of the Vanderbilt fortune find its way below the Mason and Dixon Line at a time when the rancors of the Civil War had not yet died out?

The explanation is curious and involved. The medium of transfer was a young preacher from Chapel Hill, with an unconscious assist from a Southern young lady.

"It is horrible to have no country," wrote Charles F. Deems in his diary Easter Sunday, April 16, 1865, when he got the news at Raleigh of Lee's surrender to Grant.

In December of the same year Deems, an idealistic young Methodist preacher who, at 22, had become a professor in the University of North Carolina, departed for New York where he intended to establish a weekly journal which should reconcile and unite the lately warring halves of the country. He had with him his family, a name for the paper, and $600 in cash. The paper, *The Watchman*, was soon to perish.

He was wondering what he should do next when on one Sunday he went for consolation to St. George's Episcopal Church on 15th Street, New York. When Deems sought a seat, his way was barred by the sexton, who informed him he must wait until the pew owners were seated. After waiting quite a while without a seat, Deems came away with his mind made up to have some day a church in New York where strangers would be welcomed and seats free.

Learning that New York University on Washington Square had two chapels, he hired the smaller at $25 a month, put a notice in the *Herald*, and began preaching on Sunday mornings.

Sixteen persons were present at the first service. Four Sundays later the chapel was packed. A meeting was held to organize a church "specially designed for strangers who visit the city and for particular pastoral oversight of the young men who have recently engaged in business in New York."

By January of 1868, the Church of the Strangers, as it now called itself, was strong enough to need its own edifice. Deems learned that the Mercer Street Presbyterian Church property could be had for $65,000, but he had no such sum.

About this time two ladies, evidently mother and daughter, began coming every Sunday to hear Dr. Deems, as he was now called. They were introduced to him as Mrs. Crawford and daughter "Frank" of Mobile, Ala. They were relatives of the Senator Crawford of Georgia who had once run for President.

During the summer of 1869 Miss Frank Crawford became the second wife of the millionaire, Commodore Cornelius Vanderbilt. Vanderbilt was getting old but he was still a dreaded mogul in Wall Street and the railroad world.

The newlyweds had meant to have Dr. Deems conduct the marriage ceremony but he was out of town. Although they made their home within a few blocks of the place where Dr. Deems was preaching, he did not visit them.

"I have never gone after rich people nor particularly avoided them," he wrote, "but when a man conspicuous for wealth or position desires to know me he must always seek me. That was the only thing that had kept me from visiting the Commodore and his new bride. But as soon as I discovered that it was expected, I called and was warmly welcomed. The Commodore paid me special attention. We conversed very freely, and I did not hesitate, when it was proper, to introduce the subject of religion and talk on it—I trust in a natural and proper way."

This visit to the Vanderbilt home at 10 Washington Place was followed by others, and Dr. Deems was delighted to see that the Commodore's manners were softening under the influence of his young wife.

One Saturday evening Dr. Deems dropped in at 10 Washington Place, but finding there were visitors, he stayed only a half hour. The Commodore called him into a little office that he kept beside his bedroom.

"Doctor," said the Commodore, "what is this I hear about that Mercer Street property?"

"They want $65,000," said Deems, "but I believe they will take $50,000."

"And how much of that amount have you got?" Deems felt in his pockets and said: "About 75 to 80 cents, sir, I reckon."

"How do you expect to make a payment then?"

"I shall appeal to the people of New York."

"Doctor," said the Commodore suddenly, "I'll give you the church!"

"Commodore," said the doctor, "if you give me that church for the Lord Jesus Christ, I'll most thankfully accept it."

"Don't mistake me, doctor," said Vanderbilt, "I'm not professing any religious sentiment that I don't feel. This would be from one friend to another and you are to take it that way."

Dr. Deems shook the giver's hand. "Commodore," he said, "in whatever spirit you give it, I am deeply obliged, but I shall receive it in the name of the Lord Jesus Christ."

"Oh well," said Vanderbilt, "let's go into the sitting room and see the womenfolks."

When the papers were ready, Dr. Deems called at the Commodore's office. The latter had gone to Saratoga, but a clerk handed the doctor $50,000 in a package of bills, declining to take a receipt. Dr. Deems took title, but finding the Mercer Street property much run down, he spent $5,000 on repairs. The next time he saw the Commodore, he told him about it.

"Well, Doctor," said Vanderbilt indifferently, "how are you going to pay for it?"

"I don't know, sir."

"Neither do I," said the Commodore and turned away. Deems went down to Wall Street and borrowed the money on a personal note from Charles W. Keep, a broker.

The Church of the Strangers held its first service in its new edifice on West 57th Street October 2, 1870. The great and near great often could be found in its pews.

Dr. Deems gave his members plenty to do and admire. Baptism was carried out either by total immersion in a bath built beneath the pulpit platform or by a less wholesale application of water just in front of the pulpit. A Chinese Sunday School was organized and a woman's society called Sisters of the Stranger was formed with the second Mrs. Vanderbilt as its directress.

At the end of the year 1871 Dr. Deems wrote in his diary: "My Christmas dinner was taken with my whole family at Commodore Vanderbilt's and we had a most enjoyable time." In 1873, he was able to announce that Commodore Vanderbilt had given $1,000,000 to the Central University of the Methodist Episcopal Church, South, at Nashville, Tenn., which changed its name to Vanderbilt University. In the same year, Dr. Deems bought the first home he ever owned at 429 West 22nd Street. It was not far from the high-class sporting houses for which West 23rd Street was celebrated, but Dr. Deems was satisfied and lived there 15 years.

On Thanksgiving Day, 1875, Commodore Vanderbilt, after a ride in Central Park, came down with a cold. He did not regain his strength, and though able to see his friends and talk, he spent much time in bed. Dr. Deems came to see him almost every day, although the pastor had greatly extended his enterprises, including the editing of a Sunday paper published by Frank Leslie.

Near the end the Commodore was seldom free from pain, and Deems adhered to consoling subjects. There were occasional quiet moments. In one of these the Commodore took Dr. Deems' hand and thanked him for "not crowding" religion on him. At another time the Commodore said, "Doctor, when I am gone, I want it known that I have always believed in the Bible, but on that subject you have had no more influence on me than this fan in my hand."

On December 4, 1876, Dr. Deems wrote in his diary: "Entered upon my 57th year," and just one month later he wrote: "Commodore Vanderbilt died this morning at 10:51." The funeral was held at the Church of the Strangers and the burial took place at New Dorp, Staten Island. Deems pronounced the final words. The Commodore's estate was estimated at $105,000,000. To his young wife, Frank, he bequeathed half a million in U. S. 5 per cent bonds, and the house in Washington Place. On January 8, Deems made this sole entry: "Oh, how lonely without the Commodore."

In 1877, Dr. Deems sent to Dr. Kemp P. Battle, President of the University of North Carolina, the first installment of $100 to establish a loan fund for self-help students, as a memorial to his son, Theodore Disoway Deems, who had been mortally wounded when serving under Stonewall Jackson in Virginia. He had forwarded $600 for this purpose when one day he was called to the Fifth Avenue home of William H. Vanderbilt, the late Commodore's oldest son. In the course of the conversation Mr. Vanderbilt asked about the student loan fund at Chapel Hill. Deems described it. "Here's something for it," said Mr. Vanderbilt, handing him a check. It was for $10,000. This Deems fund is still in existence and has helped hundreds of University of North Carolina students.

Dr. Deems lived actively until 1892, when a stroke deprived him of speech. He received the best care, much of it furnished at the instance of Cornelius Vanderbilt, the Commodore's grandson, but he faded away and died at the age of 73. He was buried at New Dorp, Staten Island, not far from the cemetery begun by the Vanderbilts soon after they had emigrated from Holland. The Church of the Strangers has been for many years on West 57th Street near Eighth Avenue, New York, and is in excellent condition.

The Castle Amid the Pines

Of all the sights in Chapel Hill none excites more curiosity and wonder than Gimghoul Castle, medieval in form and mysterious in air, sitting east of the campus among the pines of Point Prospect at the end of Gimghoul Road on the edge of the great plain that used to be called the Triassic Sea. The castle's origin is no less strange and romantic than its architecture, for it represents the fruition of a solitary student's dream.

Edward Wray Martin, who got his law degree here in 1891, used to walk out to Piney Prospect, as it came to be called, and gaze far out over the forest of the Triassic Sea, imagining that raising their heads from the ocean of pines and oaks were islands with unearthly names. The green area around him he called Glandon Forest, which later gave its name to the present Glandon Drive. In imagination he saw a great gloomy pile standing at the edge of the cliff that is now crowned with Dr. Battle's crescent seat. To this pile he gave the name of Hippol Castle.

Martin was a devoted reader of Arthurian and other ancient legends and saw shining knights where ordinary people saw only grey professors and fairy princesses where other people saw only fat waitresses. He related his fancies to his friends, probably never dreaming his fancies would become solid stone. But in 1915 two students, Perrin Busbee and George Stephens, members of a secret order called the Gimghouls, founded in 1889 and having a lodge on Rosemary Street, induced the order to forsake the village and buy

94 acres of faraway land at Piney Prospect. The cost was $4500.

In 1922 A. H. Patterson and T. Felix Hickerson were named on a Gimghoul committee formed to see about placing on this tract a building to be "medieval and mysterious looking." In 1924 they engaged N. C. Curtis, a University of North Carolina graduate and professional architect, to design a suitable structure. His plans were accepted and the next year Waldensian masons from Valdese, in western North Carolina, were brought in to execute them.

These men were selected not only for their competence but their historical background. The Waldenses were a European religious group, puritans and dissenters from the Roman Catholic Church, that arose in southern France on the borders of Italy about 1170 under the preaching of Peter Waldo. In 1184 they were excommunicated and subjected to a persecution that drove them to the Alps of France and Italy for refuge. A branch of them came to North Carolina, bought land in a mountainous area, on the road to Asheville, and founded a strong colony that has survived many hardships.

The Valdese masons completed the Gimghoul building and turned it over to the Order in 1926. They were paid $5,200 for their work, which was only a part of an investment that eventually came to about $50,000. Martin never saw the culmination of his dream; he died at his home in Arkansas in 1896.

Gimghoul Castle has two smaller structures as companions. One is the Battle Seat named for Dr. Kemp P. Battle, post-Civil War President of the University and for many years professor of history. He used to take long afternoon walks and was especially fond of the view at Piney

Prospect, where he would sit and rest before turning back to his home, "Senlac," built by his father, Judge William H. Battle, founder of the University law school. On each trip Dr. Battle would toss a stone on a cairn he himself had started, known as the Freshman Rock Pile. After his death in 1919 these stones were used to build the semi-circular seat to be found just below the Castle.

Closer to the Castle is a rounded boulder seeming to lift itself from the ground, around which more legends have gathered than any similar object in Chapel Hill. This is Dromgoole's Tomb. It bears spots resembling dried blood (actually iron oxide), which is supposed to have been shed by Peter Dromgoole, student, when he was killed in a duel on the spot and was buried beneath the stone. A related version declares his sweetheart, not identified except as "Miss Fanny," sickened and died soon afterward and was buried by his side. For many years a spring of clear water on the hillside was known as "Miss Fanny's Spring." A third version says that in the duel Peter killed his opponent, fled the scene, and was never heard of again.

So many variations of these legends have been passed around that at times doubt has been expressed that there was ever such a person as Peter Dromgoole. But that he existed and was a student here in 1830 to 1832 is proved by University records which show that his home was at Lawrenceville, Va. At the same address lived his uncle, George C. Dromgoole, who was a University of North Carolina student in 1814 to 1816, and also Peter's brother, Edward, who was graduated here in 1845. It was George Dromgoole who, after graduation, was involved in a duel in which he killed his opponent. This duel was wrongly attributed to Peter.

Bruce Cotten, who was a student here in 1891-92, ex-
amined the Dromgoole legends historically in 1924 and
uncovered facts that rivalled the legends. He traced the
old Dromgoole homestead to Gholsonville P. O., Brunswick
County, Va., 15 miles from Roanoke Rapids, N. C. It was
the home of the Rev. Edward Dromgoole, grandfather of
Peter. Edward was an Irishman born in Sligo and though a
Roman Catholic, became on reaching the United States a
Methodist minister.

His grandson Peter was born February 8, 1815, in Halifax
County, N. C. At 18 he tried to enter the University but on
January 1 he wrote his father he had been "rejected" at
Chapel Hill, presumably because of faulty preparation.
Nevertheless he remained on the campus, possibly in the
preparatory department, and March 1, 1833, wrote that he
was "very well satisfied with the Hill of Science."

It is part of the Peter Dromgoole legend that at this
period he was rather "wild," but his room-mate, John Huxton
Williams of Warren County, reported him well-behaved
and well-liked. Peter's father may have heard rumors of his
wildness and may have written him a letter whose sting
Peter resented, for on April 8, 1833, he wrote home dra-
matically:

"I have determined never more to see that parent's face
whom I have treated with so little respect . . . I shall sail for
Europe never to return again."

Another letter, the last one received from him at Chapel
Hill, so alarmed his mother that she begged his uncle, George
C. Dromgoole, to go there and investigate. George did so
and on May 7, 1833, wrote from Raleigh that Peter had said
nothing to Williams about his proposed departure, that he

had left behind his trunk, books, and most of his clothes, and that Williams, a former room-mate, had declared Peter had "conducted himself with propriety and was respected by the students."

From Peter no word has ever come back.

The Rev. James Pleasant Mason and His Three Loves

I

The Rev. James Pleasant Mason had three loves. One was the 800-acre farm near Chapel Hill on which he and his wife lived for many years. The other two were his teen-age daughters, Martha and Varina, whose portraits hang in a building on the campus of the University of North Carolina by dint of a curious provision in a will, although they were not students of the University and had no actual connection with it.

To record the events on his farm and the daily activities of his daughters, Mr. Mason in 1876 started a diary which eventually filled nearly 15 small volumes. It is a chronicle of the period and of the progress of his three great loves. He had a fourth love, though a minor one. That was his service to half a dozen country churches situated well beyond the periphery of the village of Chapel Hill. He gave this service faithfully, but his entries relating to these churches were mostly businesslike and perfunctory, for at heart he was not a preacher but a farmer and a father.

He also had at times the feelings of a psalmist. For example, on June 29, 1880, he found the first cotton blossom of the year followed by, wrote he, "a sweet rain for which we do thank the Lord."

His daily entries regarding his farm operations were dominated by references to rain. Rain was the life giver. Its presence or absence determined the day's work and shaped the employment of all hands. Its signs were the first thing to be looked for on rising in the morning and on closing the house doors at night. It colored human thought in terms of hymns of praise to the Almighty or of resignation to the divine will. Showers or promising clouds gave his diary a genial glow, but barren days could only make him write: "dry, dry, dry."

Hearty rain had a triple meaning. It not only brought needed moisture to seeds and roots, but it filled the creek so that cotton could be run through the water-power gin, and finally it freshened the streams in which converts could be baptized, for Mr. Mason as a devout Baptist believed in total immersion. He sometimes presided or assisted at the baptizing of as many as 40 persons in ceremonies that filled the best part of a day.

Cotton and corn: these were the two crops that absorbed most of the Mason farm's labor. They sold cheaply, cotton at around ten cents a pound, and corn, though if ground was used for bread, was thought of as the proper food for pigs. It was a long time before Southern farmers realized these two cheap crops made for a cheap life.

Preachers, like other things in Mr. Mason's day and region, came cheap. For instance, he records that on a day in 1876, he received $18 on salary account and a payment of $31 previously. Such remittances forced ministers like Mr. Mason to bolster their earnings by labors other than serving churches. But work on the farm, no matter how exacting, he regarded as no hardship. On the contrary, he found satisfaction and even pleasure in every phase of labor on the land, even though it necessitated rising in the morning before day and having breakfast by lamplight and even though his duties brought on him certain risks.

For instance, he was summoned one day to Lystra, a country church south of Chapel Hill, to preach a funeral. His means of transportation, as often, was a horse. But enroute the horse bucked and threw him. Nevertheless he reached the church, his diary doesn't say how, and preached the funeral. While he was recovering from his injury his wife Mary kept his diary and made daily entries in a delicate feminine hand contrasting strongly with his own heavy lettering.

Mary was governed by a devotion to duty. If there was a gap to fill in life on the farm, she filled it as far as a woman's strength permitted, and while her husband was away on pastoral duties she stayed at home and cooked, washed, sewed, mended, managed the children, waited on guests and directed the servants. She was not a good companion to her husband. She had no time to be.

Mary was the great-granddaughter of Mark Morgan, an old settler who came down from Pennsylvania in the late 18th Century and bought a tract of land of about 1600 acres near Chapel Hill that had been a part of the Granville Grant. This land lay on both sides of the creek which eventually bore his name and which was lined with huge sycamore trees. One of them, a hollow, was so big that legend said Morgan had parked his wife in it while he built a more substantial shelter for her. His donation of 107 acres was among the original gifts of land that had determined the founding of the University of North Carolina at Chapel Hill.

At Mark's death Mary inherited 800 acres, part of it rising ground and part a level loam, that became a rich and productive farm when she married the Rev. James Pleasant Mason of an old Orange County rural family. He had a zeal for land and under his management the farm prospered and often drew visitors from the village of Chapel Hill and from the University faculty, for its hospitality was boundless and its woods and fields pleasant like his middle name. Yet there was something spare about its big house, for its mistress and master had both come from a sparse existence.

One of the visitors who often came to the Mason Farm was Cornelia Phillips Spencer, historian, teacher to the Mason children, sister of University professors, and often used as consultant by Mr. Mason himself. On a June day soon after the Civil War's end she wrote in her journal:

"I walked with Miss Nancy Hilliard, Jane Cave, and (daughter) June down to Reverend Mr. Mason's to spend the day . . . Here are people who have had an independent and handsome property for years, living without any but the simplest comforts of life. 'Comforts'—I don't call five, or eight, or even 10 great feather beds in such weather as this comforts—not a chair but a *split* bottom in the house. Not a fork but a two pronged one. Not six tumblers. Not a set of table-ware of any sort. Not a carpet, nor a curtain, nor a napkin. Not one single article of luxury in the house."

This spare existence was somewhat mitigated when the children came and began to grow up. There were four originally. Two survived: Martha (Mattie), born in 1857, and Varina, born in 1861. Both were fond of social life and liked to have visitors come, stay late, and spend the night. There were ample rooms and beds for that purpose.

II

When these two girls reached their teens, life for their father received a decided spur. They liked to go into Chapel

Hill, something over two miles distant, to attend church and
Sunday School, to listen to lectures, and to sample other
University attractions, and to be tutored by Mrs. Spencer,
who taught them literature, history, botany, the arts, and
even mathematics, in which her older brother, Charles, and
father, James, were professors. To make these visits to the
village the girls had to have an escort—their father was a
ready one—and a conveyance. This was a light carriage
called a rockaway. In these town trips Mr. Mason learned to
take great delight. He sometimes went on horseback, a half
hour each way. He came to know many faculty people and
it pleased him when he saw how readily they responded to
invitations from him and his daughters. Among them was
Dr. Charles Phillips and his wife, Laura. Mrs. Spencer often
came out to the farm, sometimes on foot, accompanied by
her daughter, June. The Patterson brothers, H. H. ("Hoot"),
the merchant prince of the village, and Wiley T., the University Bursar, were frequent visitors. Once the young professor, E. A. Alderman, escorted the girls home after an
evening entertainment in the village and spent the night.
"Dr. Ed," as he was called, was a lively and humorous companion, but he had his serious side, and no one thought his
elevation was undeserved when he became President of the
University of North Carolina; and when, remarkably, he
went on to become President of Tulane University and
finally of the University of Virginia.

Besides professors and townsmen there were any number of visiting preachers, all of whom enjoyed chicken
dinners and fresh vegetables from the Mason garden while
they had hours of churchly gossip. One of these clerical
visitors was the Rev. George W. Purefoy, who owned the
mill bearing his name and a farm that was so completely

raided near the end of the Civil War by the hangers-on of
Gen. W. T. Sherman's Federal Army, known as "Sherman's
Bummers," that the neighbors had to join to find food
enough for his family. His name is preserved by Purefoy
Road, on the south side of Chapel Hill.

III

The Mason daughters found the most attractive and
virile of these visitors to be the young Baptist preacher,
the Rev. A. C. Dixon. About 1878 he came so often to the
Mason home, on church business of course, that the gossips
maintained he had interests there other than religious ones,
and they speculated as to which of the Mason daughters
would eventually be his choice as a wife, since they were
nubile and healthy girls, and it was fitting that a minister
have a good wife. But Mr. Dixon (a brother of Thomas
Dixon, author of *The Klansman*) had his own ideas and
disappointed the gossips. After several months his name disappeared from the Mason diary and it was revealed that he
had not only left the community but the country. He had
sailed for England where he became pastor of the great
Baptist Temple in London.

The Mason home also attracted lesser fry. They came
to sell goods or services, but remained to stay for a hearty
meal and often to spend the night in one of Mrs. Mason's
enormous feather beds. Among them were spectacle salesmen, book agents, portrait salesmen, and pack peddlers with
novelties for the ladies. Somehow they all seemed to arrive
at the Mason home about an hour before the evening meal
and after displaying their goods and receiving their orders,
it was time for dinner, to which, in accord with the laws of
hospitality, they were always invited and which they always

accepted with alacrity. And then after dinner, they could hardly be expected to take to the road again in darkness and perhaps bad weather, and so they were invited to spend the night, which they did with one accord.

It was probably about this time in Mr. Mason's 50th year that Mrs. Spencer, who had a ready pen, wrote concerning Mr. Mason that as a pastor he preached "acceptably, being plain, lively and warm." He was a man of sprightly and in-quisitive disposition, always cheerfully and amiably disposed, fond of reading and intelligently interested in public men and matters. He was also a successful farmer; by his good management he doubled the value of his wife's estate.

IV

About Mrs. Mason she was more reserved. "Mrs. Mason," she wrote, "had had few advantages in her youth—having spent half of her life in attendance on the lingering illness of parents, brothers and sisters . . . They owned a number of slaves but such service was never required of negroes. When Mrs. Mason was not by a sick bed she was weaving and making the clothing required for the family, white and colored. The delights of literature, of society, of youth outings or pleasures of any sort, were pretty well unknown to her till after her marriage when her children began to grow up. But she stood in her lot and performed her round of hard and narrow duty faithfully. Once towards the close of her life, I, holding her hand, remarked on its extreme softness and delicacy of texture and said to her jocularly: 'I don't believe you have ever done any work in your life.' She replied seriously, 'You are wrong; these hands have woven and made up hundreds of yards of cloth.' She told me once that for years before her marriage she never knew what it was even to get to church.

". . . When a woman living two or three miles from every where, in the country, with roads almost impassable in the winter season, could not get to church, or to a camp meeting, and had no books, nor papers nor magazines, and hardly any neighbors, what was she to do but spin and sew, and knit, attend to the butter making and raising of poultry? The possession of slaves and of many broad acres made but little difference in the way of life between those who had and those who had not. The men could always mount their horses and ride off for the day—to church or to court; or perhaps 'twas election day or a big sale that called them. The woman stayed at home and kept affairs there on the track. And it is everlasting testimony to the value of such homely life and home duties well performed with careful consideration of the nature of things, that these stay-at-home women were always found to be able to hold their own, exhibited sense and judgment, and capacity for business quite equal to their husbands! Mrs. Mason was a silent woman, reserved, and inclined to brood over 'old far off unhappy things.' She thought and felt more deeply than her husband, and having once made up her mind she adhered to it. He asked and deferred to her judgment continually."

Mrs. Spencer mentioned in the same letter to Dr. Kemp P. Battle in 1894, when she was living with her daughter June (Mrs. James Lee Love) at 27 Wallace St., Cambridge, Mass., that the Masons were ambitious for Mattie and Varina and fully agreed that "they should have every opportunity that their means could afford for education and for all the good that comes of education. For twenty years this was their one purpose."

When they chose Mrs. Spencer as preceptor for their daughters they chose the person in Chapel Hill best qualified to be a teacher of impressionable young girls. She wrote:

"From the winter of 1869-70 I saw these girls daily for five years, teaching them with my own daughter and leading them along to make pleasant acquaintance with the beginning of a good education. They were not of what Dr. Holmes distinguishes as 'literary blood,'—but they had a hereditary disposition to take pains and do their duty. They soon learned to love reading and explore for hid treasures in other languages than their own, a certain humility and docility of disposition served them well in the absence of more brilliant qualities. They finished their school days at the Baptist Female Institute in Raleigh under the care of Prof. F. P. Hobgood, and there too they both became members of the Baptist church, receiving baptism at the hands of the Rev. Dr. Pritchard.

"Their lives at home for a few short years were ideal in their relations to their parents, to each other and to their few intimate associates. The old family slaves had mostly clung to the old plantation and to them their 'young mistisses,' as they called them, were objects of deepest interest and fond affection. It was pretty to see an old nurse pull one of them down upon her knees and talk to her as if she was still a child. 'Aunt Jane,' said Varina to her old nurse one day, 'I never see you but I feel as if I want to get in your lap and have a good cry.'

"The simplicity and ingenuousness of childhood marked them in everything. Reading aloud well was one of the accomplishments of Varina and she delighted in it for the amusement of the family. She would close her piano or lay

aside her own work with alacrity to read for hours to an
invalid visitor, and she opened in this way a new world to
her mother, who learned to enjoy sermons, works of fiction,
and newspapers for the first time in her life, a resource for
her mind that proved invaluable when she was bereft of her
children. Neither of the girls would hesitate to take a long
walk over hill and dale to secure for a friend a perfect
specimen of some rare wild flower, the fringed gentian, the
sabbatia or the fragrant wintergreen. These walks, these
wild woods, the rushing stream, the laurel, the kalmia, and
the yellow jessamine that hung over it were indeed among
their best teachers and friends. These two sisters, whose
names are to be henceforth indissolubly connected with our
State University, were emphatically good girls, intelligent,
sincere, modest, and pious."

V

Mr. Mason's diary was begun in 1876. On January 4 he
had a trip to make to Raleigh. Since Chapel Hill had no
railway connections such a journey was complicated and
exhausting. He left the farm at eight that morning and
driving a buggy, started for Morrisville, a hamlet on the
railroad 19 miles distant. It took him four hours to make the
journey, and then he had to wait until 3:00 p.m. for "the
cars," as trains were then called. The rest was fairly easy.
He reached Raleigh at four that afternoon. Altogether the
trip of 30 miles occupied eight hours.

Largely to blame was the condition of the secondary
roads, which in midwinter were mostly mud. On this
journey to Raleigh the buggy suffered a mishap, for on the
following Sunday he found on a visit to Cane Creek, one

of the country churches he served, that it was "badly broken." A local smith repaired it and charged 40 cents.

Cane Creek Church was the center that spring of several events, one of which was sensational. This was the arraignment of "quite a number" for "dancing and drunkenness." To offset this shocking episode, 42 persons from Cane Creek came forward that spring to be baptized at Thompson's Mill. The community, however, was not free from Satan's wiles, for Mr. Mason records that Bethel Church, closer to Chapel Hill, had turned out five persons for drunkenness, and that "old Mr. J. D." had been "excluded from the church," cause not specified.

Cane Creek got one more entry that spring. This involved a theological argument, but the details were not given. Mr. Mason merely wrote: "I had a warm discussion with a Methodist and his wife." It might be guessed that the debate had to do with the question of authority vs. independence. In the Methodist system the higher authorities ruled; but in the Baptist system each church congregation was independent and not subject to orders from a bishop or other authority.

As the spring of 1876 ripened, the diary naturally carried many references to the weather, and Mr. Mason noted on some days there was "a thundering around." He had another odd phrase often used—"fixed off." In recording preparation and starting for a long trip, sometimes of a day's length, he would write: "I fixed off for Raleigh." Although normally of a cheerful disposition, he occasionally indicted himself for "fretting." Once after upsetting his ink bottle, he wrote at bedtime: "I ask pardon for fretting and now retire to try to pray, feel better, retire at 9, slept only tolerable."

Summer came and on June 22, 1876, he wrote: "Varina is 15 years old." Rena, as she was called, was the younger and more favored daughter. She was more animated than her dignified sister Mattie, and her father was responsive to her every desire. After this June boundary had been passed the two girls began to go oftener to Chapel Hill. They were already well acquainted there, due to their daily schooling by Mrs. Spencer. Now they went to the University village two or three evenings every week; for life at their country home was humdrum, its duties were fixed, and all the boys were on the campus, two and a half miles distant. So they went to church, to mid-week prayer meeting, to lectures and debates, to political and social gatherings, and gladly accepted invitations to spend the night with town families. Their conveyance was called a "rockaway." Their father never balked at escorting them on Chapel Hill visits, though this often necessitated a round trip by day, another at night, and still another to bring the girls back next morning.

A break in this schedule occurred in the summer of 1877 when the University opened a summer Normal School for teachers and thus admitted women as students, although for a severly limited period and under sharp restrictions. Women who attended were known as "normals"; many of them learned to take walks to the Mason home and accept its hospitality. The opening of this school imparted a freer atmosphere to the town and campus, and delighted the Mason girls. They could now go into the village daily, attend lectures where there were plenty of people, and meet interesting persons other than Baptist ministers who were usually solid men but a trifle dull to a teen-age girl.

The year ended with two entries in the diary. One said: "I put on my flannel shirt," and the other noted that cotton, on which the farm was partly dependent, sold for 10.25 to 10.87 cents a pound. This was a low price, but not as low as that which prevailed a few years later, when cotton sank to five cents a pound. Many was the small cotton farmer who all but broke his back and injured his health by desperate efforts to break even and care for his family on so wretched an income, causing cotton to be known as a "poverty crop." At this period Mr. Mason often recorded the poor state of his health; he suffered from headaches and sore throat. He sometimes found it more profitable to haul his cotton the 30 miles to Raleigh and barter it for fertilizer than to accept the local market price.

Farm work was often interrupted by pastoral duties. For instance, on a bleak morning early in January, 1878, he was awakened before daylight by a message that a member of one of his country congregations had hanged himself during the night, and that Mr. Mason was expected to come and preach the funeral. He wrote: "I went. Took breakfast there."

On March 13, 1878, he recorded his 51st birthday, and wrote that he had been honored when Mrs. Spencer came out from Chapel Hill and spent the day. "The Lord be praised," he added, "for his mercy to me."

A year later he wrote: "I am this day 52 years old and call upon my soul and all that is within me to praise and thank the Lord for his long suffering toward me." Shortly afterward he wrote: "Beautiful clear day. Went to pig pen to work but pigs got out." No details given nor were there any when he had to note among other mishaps on the farm: "Lucy Phillips got hurt on the Mill hill. Brought her to stay all night. Took her home next day." She was a professor's daughter and niece of Mrs. Spencer. She was also the author's mother.

On the last day of the year 1878 he wrote: "Blessed be the name of the Lord for his goodness to us all." His next sentence said: "Looks like rain all afternoon." His first entry of the new year said: "Lord, may I live through this year and do some good." The next week he wrote: "Varina went to the Methodist church to hear a woman (Mrs. Moon) preach. I and the girls went at night. I am not in favor of a woman preaching."

Not all farmers take much notice of nature, or the works of nature, around them, nor does Mr. Mason's diary indicate he had the time to note such things except the state of the weather. But on May 20, 1879, he made one conspicuous observation: "Found five partridge nests, all having eggs in them. Took 58 eggs." Partridge was the almost universal name at this time for the bird that was later called quail or bobwhite. This tribe of birds flourished on the Mason farm until recent times when repeating shotguns and poachers cut them down.

In mid-summer of this year began a drought that lasted five weeks, causing a deep despondency in the diarist. "Dry, dry, dry," he wrote day after day, and in country churches there were repeated prayers for rain. At last on July 29 he was able to write: "We went to church, came back, and took dinner at Ruffin Whitaker's. Got caught in a fine rain after we passed through Chapel Hill. The first to wet much since first June." This end of a long drought filled the country streams so that public baptism could be resumed, and he wrote:

"Went to Thompson's mill pond and baptized eleven (11) persons, returned to church, preached to a very large audience and closed one of the most interesting meetings I ever conducted. I came home by sunset. Hadn't been home since a week ago yesterday." At the end of this year he made this entry: "I humbly thank the Lord for the many blessings he has given us through the year now closing. Not a physician has been called to see one on the farm except Dr. Ward to see me January 7." On his birthday in the following March he wrote in a similar strain, saying: "I am this day 53 years old. I do thank the Lord for preserving my life so long. I pray the Lord to enable me to give him my heart and life the remaining days which He may see fit to allow me to live."

Fifty-three does not seem to mark an unusually long human life. But at this period the life of a Southern farmer was too filled with grinding toil to enable him to survive very far beyond his fiftieth year. In addition, he often had to live amid unsanitary conditions. In fact, Mr. Mason had barely recorded his thankfulness for a year of good health for all on the farm when he had to note that "Dr. Mallett came to see Mattie, stayed all night." In the early spring of 1880 Varina began to go into the village alone to take music lessons, and thereafter she and her sister Mattie began to resort to separate ways and seldom went out together. Later in the year Mattie went alone to Raleigh to visit friends and was gone for six weeks.

The seeking by the girls of other interests than those of the farm caused the Masons to draw together more closely for counsel and support, and thereafter Mr. Mason's diary was more frequent in its mention of Mrs. Mason. In fact, on July 26, 1880, it recorded a momentous event. This was the approach of the railroad to Chapel Hill, which had been without a rail connection since its inception and which had heretofore been approachable only by some horse-drawn vehicle moving at hardly more than four miles an hour. This meant that persons traveling between the State capital and Chapel Hill had to calculate that at least four hours would be required for the journey, while Durham, which was comparatively near, was two hours distant.

The line connecting the University with the outside world was only a branch spur, reaching the main line between Durham and Greensboro at a rural point called University Station. This name misled travellers from a distance and confused even the natives, for when they bought tickets to University, N. C., supposing trains would deposit them in Chapel Hill on the edge of the campus, they were disconcerted to learn that they might have to wait hours for the Chapel Hill one-lung train, meantime having only the pines and katydids for company.

A prized joke depicted a University professor returning home after an absence. His seat on the tooter, which was late, was behind that of a lady who was evidently a stranger. When in the darkness the little train stopped with a sudden jerk, the lady turned and exclaimed in alarm: "I wonder what has happened." Said the professor soothingly: "I think, ma'am, the engineer has got out to inquire the way."

VI

At the end of this year the Mason diary carried this bold comment: "This has been the best year to me and family for many years past." On the first day of the new year, 1881, he wrote: I commence this diary praying that I may write something good on every page."

He had no means of knowing that this year would be momentous, and that 1881 and its events would never die out of his memory. It did not begin auspiciously. Varina came down with measles, cotton at Durham sold down to 9¾ cents, and up to the middle of June rain had been stingy, "Not enough to drop from the eaves." Varina recovered from the measles but did not seem to gather strength. July brought a high and languorous heat. Mr. Mason exchanged some of it for heat in Washington, D. C., where he visited Samuel F. Phillips, former Chapel Hillian who had been Solicitor General in President Grant's administration. (See chapter on "Mr. Sam and His Stucco House.")

On Mr. Mason's return he found that Varina, his favorite daughter, had been confined to bed for several days and that Dr. Mallett, the village's chief physician, had been calling on her daily. On August 23 the doctor visited Varina twice in one day and spent three successive nights near her bedside, making 19 visits in succession. On September 4, he called in Dr. J. C. Patterson for consultation. The next day Mr. Mason asked for their opinion. Their reply was, "We still hope." That night Mr. Mason spent what his diary recorded as "the most dreadful night of my life." At daybreak, September 6, Varina died. She was buried at 5 p.m. the same day. She was 20 years old.

Her father was at first steady in his demeanor and the very next day made his usual matter-of-fact entry in his diary, saying "A very hot day. Sent broken wagon wheel to shop this evening." A week later the other daughter, Mattie, went to Chapel Hill and was gone five days. On her return she said she was not feeling well and went to bed. Dr. Harris, the University physician, was sent for. A few days later Mr. Mason sent a hurry call to Dr. Harris at 9 p.m. He came and stayed all night. That visit gave the parents cause for alarm, but in a few days Mattie was well enough to ride a horse over to visit some neighbors. Mr. Mason felt he could ease his tension and went fishing. He caught a turtle and brought it home for conversion into turtle soup.

The third week in October came, a period when the air and leafage at Chapel Hill are at their finest. On the night of the 21st Mr. Mason looked at his daughter at 2:30 a.m. and at once sent an urgent message to Dr. Harris, who came and spent the night, returning the next night and the next. He called to see Mattie 17 times in succession and then called Dr. Roberson for consultation. There were no entries in the Mason diary for eight days and then he recorded that Dr. Harris had paid a long delayed visit to his home in the village. On Nov. 23, 1881, Mattie died.

Mr. and Mrs. Mason had thus lost their two daughters within a period of about ten weeks. Both were victims of typhoid fever, a malady that often beset rural and village homes of the day. Doctors knew little of either preventive or curative measures. Mattie was 24 years old. The day after her funeral, her father made no entry in his diary. But the farm and its life had to go on and the next day he wrote in his little book: "Killed hogs. Cut up and salted the next day." A few days later he recorded that three more hogs had been killed, weighing 331, 362, and 371 pounds, making a total of more than 1000 pounds. He tried valiantly to keep affairs on the farm moving, but before the month was out he had to write in his diary just two words, "Right sick."

He was not aware of it, but in the death of his two daughters he had suffered a trauma from which he would not soon recover. In his diary for several days there were only blanks. When he had gathered a little strength he requested President Battle to come out and write wills for himself and Mrs. Mason. The loss of his two daughters brought him closer to Mrs. Mason, and he began to take buggy rides with her, occasionally going as far as Durham. But at this period there was no life in the diary he kept. For days the entries were confined to one or two lines. One of them recorded on the last day of the year that he had ginned 56 bales of cotton in 1880, "the dryest year," he wrote, "ever known."

On the first day of the new year, 1882, he mentioned a snowfall and then wrote: "The Lord be praised for sparing me so long. I pray the Lord for his blessing this year. I don't wish to peer into the future, but as my days so may my strength be." This entry was written in three different inks, indicating it was not put down all at one time. And then he collapsed. Dr. Roberson called to see him daily, succeeded by Dr. Mallett who watched over him all that spring. A single notation in his diary said he had been having a "long hard spell." Then the diary remained blank until the end of March when he wrote: "Stepped on the ground today, the first time since the first week in January." By April 25 he had rallied somewhat and wrote: "Commenced planting cotton seed at 11 a.m." He added: "I have been stirring about since April 1. But oh, what a fearful blank preceding."

On May 2 he wrote that the branch railroad line to Chapel Hill had been finished but he was not able to join in the celebration that ensued. He tried to drive into the village in his buggy, but turned around and came home. All that summer he was repeatedly attended by Drs. Roberson, Mallett, and MacNider. The evidence is that his weakness was due to typhoid fever, the same malady that had carried off his daughters, and this weakness lasted until the first of October, 1882, when he resumed his diary, writing: "Beau-

tiful bright day. Went to church in Chapel Hill, called on
Dr. (Charles) Phillips."

By the middle of October he was stronger and his interest
in outdoor life returned. On the 14th he recorded that wild
geese had passed over, and then ensued a period when he
and his wife Mary took daily walks about the farm. This
period of partial recovery reached a climax on Nov. 16, 1882,
when he was able to go to Raleigh by starting from Chapel
Hill on the new branch railroad line. This journey must
have been exhilarating, for previously, as mentioned, a round
trip to Raleigh, which was his market center, occupied almost an entire day and necessitated long buggy or horseback
rides.

An unusual visitor at this time was Col. L. L. Polk,
leader of the Populist movement and editor of a farm journal. Mr. Mason's physical tone continued to rise and by
Christmas Day he was able to record it as a "calm sweet
day," while the next day he described as "exceedingly beautiful."

On New Year's Day, 1883, when snow lay on the ground,
he wrote: "The Lord be praised and grant us precious blessings all this year or while we live." On March 13 his entry
said: "This day I am 56 years old. How good the Lord has
been to me to spare my life so long." On April 26 he recorded frost, which was very unusual, and so was the delay
in planting corn until May 8.

In the middle of July he went to Raleigh where his
diary said he had "bought monuments." These no doubt
included the shaft which was put up over his daughters'
graves, where they lay side by side a hundred yards below
the house, on Oct. 24, 1883, in a copse of cedars and hollies

intact today; and also possibly included the stones which were to mark the graves of himself and wife.

On Thanksgiving Day, 1883, he and his wife had a "fatted 'possum" for dinner. In the afternoon Cornelia Phillips Spencer called and he proudly showed her 15 fatted hogs. "They're pretty and that's a fact," said Mrs. Spencer, which comment he recorded in the diary. That evening he wrote down his feelings: "Much has been taken from us, but I still have much to be thankful for. Restored health, a good home, a faithful wife, still a good hope through grace."

As the old year expired he hitched up his horses to haul some logs to the sawmill, but they balked and he had to take them out and put mules, which are not temperamental, in their stead, illustrating one of the thousand difficulties in operating a farm.

The new year of 1884 he signalized by taking the honey from four stands of bees. When his birthday came in March he wrote: "I heartily pray the Lord to forgive my sins of 57 years." A few days later he recorded a visit from June Spencer, daughter of Cornelia Phillips Spencer. June was about to sail for Europe. She was accompanied to the dock by Prof. James Lee Love, to whom she was subsequently married. Later that year Mr. Mason recorded a visit from a "specs man," meaning a vendor of eye-glasses, and bought from him glasses for his wife and himself at $15 each.

The beginning of 1885 found Mr. Mason too "poorly" to keep up his diary. When warm weather came he went to Buffalo Lithia Springs for a rest but had a severe chill there (indicating malaria as well as typhoid?) and had to return home without improvement. The last day of the year was noteworthy for his failure to write in his diary his prayers and gratitude to the Almighty. In fact, he did not thus use his diary again until his birthday in 1891 when he wrote: "I do humbly thank God for preserving me so long. I have been so great a sinner." In the next few years he had little to chronicle except references to his ill health and occasional sickness of his wife, Mary. They were both pleased by visits from such University professors as Battle, Gore, Toy, Winston and the University physician, Dr. Whitehead. The latter liked to hunt quail and bathe in Morgan Creek. Most frequent visitor of all was Mrs. Spencer who wrote Mrs. Charles Phillips: "My poor Mr. and Mrs. Mason are an instance of how the broken heart can live on and find something to live for."

Their strength waned, but in 1893 Mr. Mason rallied enough to be able to write in his diary on March 13: "I am this day 66 years old. The Lord be praised for his long suffering. Blessed be his holy name for not cutting me down long since as a cumberer of the earth." On June 21, 1893, he made an entry about getting some plowing done. Three days later he died quietly. His wife lived a year longer until July, 1894. They were buried in the little plot below the house that had been prepared 10 years before. The inscription above his grave read:

"James Pleasant Mason, born March 13, 1827, died June 24, 1893. For forty years a faithful minister of the Baptist Church. In labors abundant, in weariness and painfulness. Light is given to him that was in misery." Her grave was inscribed: *"Mary Elizabeth, daughter of Solomon P. Morgan and wife of Rev. J. P. Mason. Born February 16, 1825. Died July 17, 1894. Resigned to God's will under many afflictions. He maketh sore and bindeth up. He woundeth and his hands make whole."*

Their joint will bequeathed the Mason farm and $1000

in money to the University of North Carolina, with the provision that $15 be spent annually to keep in order the plot in which the parents and two daughters were buried and that portraits of the two girls and their father be painted and preserved in University halls. The girls' portraits were painted by Mary Graves Rees, sister of Louis Graves, long the editor of the village's one newspaper. The portrait of their father reproduced in this volume was painted by W. G. Randall, the "po' boy" artist whose story is told on other pages of this book. The little cemetery in which all are buried lies under the copse of hollies and cedars on the south side of the golf clubhouse at the farm.

Index